SCALES & TALES

A Beginner's Guide to Fantasy Role-Playing Games

Kevin Sherry

Andrews McMeel
PUBLISHING®

CONTENTS

How to Use This Book   1

Time to Play! 55

The Conclusion 121

HOW TO USE THIS BOOK

This book is everything you'll need to start playing a fantasy adventure game! One player (probably you) will be the GAME MASTER or GM. That person is supposed to read this entire book and will have a good grasp of the rules, so they can show the other players as you go along.

The Game Master

The GM is responsible for telling the story and setting up the game board and terrain. They will be acting as all the opposing monsters and characters in the story. The GM is not playing against the players. The GM is controlling the flow of the game and making sure the whole party has a good time.

The GM will ideally have four people to play the Heroes. These players will create their own characters and participate in the quests the GM presents.

To play *Scales & Tales*, ideally you would have ten six-sided dice (d6) and two twenty-sided dice (d20). However, you could make do with one of each. Ask players to bring their own lucky dice.

Note: If you have less than four Heroes, it's OK to lessen the number of Enemies or even let the players carry more spells or gear. You want the players to have fun!

Tabletop Gaming

Scales & Tales can be played as a free-form tabletop game or on top of a grid. When playing on a table, players use miniature figurines to represent the Heroes and their Enemies, and the GM uses different matcrials to represent the terrain, buildings, dungeons, and greenery.

A standard grid uses one-inch squares. At this scale, one inch represents five feet in real life.

Important: Only draw or represent what the Heroes would be seeing. Don't reveal rooms, scenery, and terrain until the Heroes get to those areas in the game.

Pro Tip: Using a laminated washable grid for the game board and drawing the terrain with a washable marker is the easiest way to represent the world around them in a visual sense. It will still require all the players to use their imagination, but it gives a clear idea of where the game is happening.

Terrain

Stone or wood blocks can be used as castle walls. Some people carve foam to represent hills and craters.

Peat moss and hobby moss can be used as trees or thick brush. Succulents like small cacti can be used as large trees.

You can also use items from other games or things you might find in a thrift store.

Miniatures

Miniatures can be used to represent Heroes, Enemies, and other creatures on the board. For normal-sized creatures and Heroes, your miniatures should be small enough to fit inside a one-inch square in order to keep everything on the board to scale.

Paper and Coin Method

This is a really easy and fun way to represent your character or any other creature or monster within the game.

Pro tip: Cardstock or an index card are more durable than regular paper.

Snacks

You'll be sitting around the table with some of your friends for a couple of hours, so you should provide some food and drinks, or make it a potluck where everyone brings food.

Finger foods are usually best so you don't get your books, drawings, or miniatures greasy or slimy with sauce!

How to Role-Play

In a fantasy role-playing game, a player creates a character who will be their avatar. They will be this character during the game, including acting and speaking like that character would speak. This character is placed in an imaginary world that is created by the Game Master (GM).

The players then explore the fantasy world of the game, and the GM keeps them entertained (or terrified) by leading them through a story, telling them about the environment, posing puzzles and riddles, and challenging them with Enemies in combat.

In *Scales & Tales* and most RPGs, a character can do two things during their turn.

Movement Phase: During your turn, a Hero or Enemy can move up to their full movement score. Taking one step is free.

Action Phase: A Hero can explore the world around them and do almost anything during this phase.

Examples:

Combat
Casting a spell
Searching for secrets
Picking a lock
Searching for treasure
Healing
Reading a scroll
Passing an item to another Hero
Composing themselves after a big hit
Eating something
Making a diversion
Interviewing someone/thing
Climbing a tree or wall
Setting a trap
Making a fire
Setting up a camp
Searching for a Familiar
. . . etc.

Double Up: You can move twice as far but make no action, or you can stay where you are and do two actions.

Creating Characters

The first thing you will do as a group is create your Heroes by filling out your character sheets.

On that character sheet, first you will randomly determine your character's Hero Trait scores.

The Hero Traits are Power, Skill, and Wit. Every action you take within the world of *Scales & Tales* can be tested against these three Traits.

First Things First: For each of the three Hero Traits, roll three six-sided dice and add those numbers together. Record the total and then move to the next Trait. At the end, the players will have three numbers between three and eighteen.

Character Sheet Key

HP – Hit Points. This is the amount of life that a Hero has. Getting attacked or hurt can lower this number, while potions, spells, and healing can raise this number.

Low Life — When they take more damage points than their HP, they will need to take a break from playing to revive themselves to the health of one.

> **Example:** If Hero Penny with an HP of 2 is blasted by a fireball that deals 4 damage, Penny would end up at 0 life. Penny would be passed the next time it would be her turn. At the beginning of her next turn, her HP would be 1.

XP – Experience Points. When you do anything especially awesome or creative, the GM will award you one or more points of XP. If you get 10 XP, you can LEVEL UP to become more powerful.

Catchphrase – A catchphrase makes your character more memorable. This can also be developed over the course of the game; you don't have to start with one. Think of some of your favorite catchphrases from pop culture. "It's GO time," "Up, up, and AWAY!," or change an existing expression, such as "Break a leg" or "Toot your own horn," to suit your character.

Backpack Items – The number of items you carry in your backpack depends on your Hero Type.

Hands – You can only hold one or two things with your two hands.

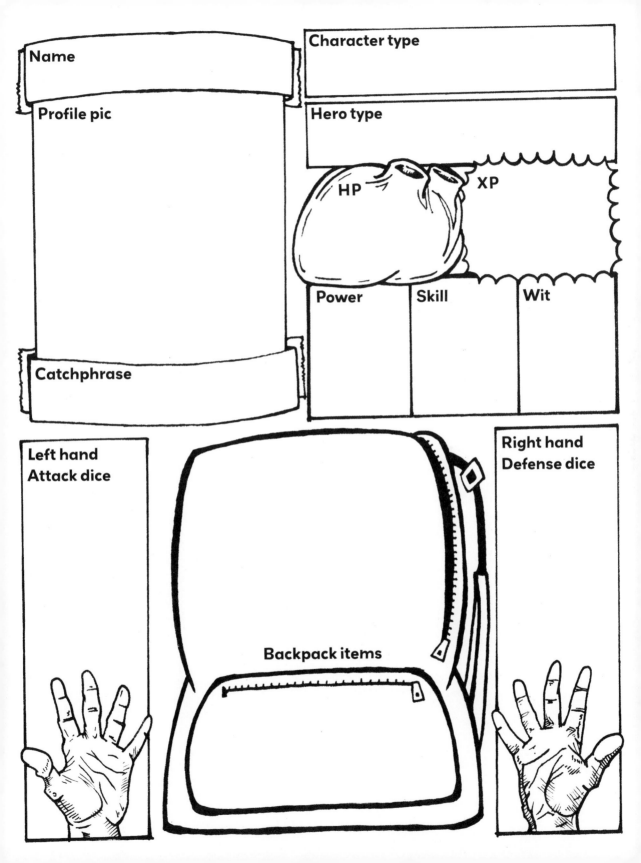

Name

Profile pic

Catchphrase

Character type

Hero type

HP

XP

Power

Skill

Wit

Left hand
Attack dice

Right hand
Defense dice

Backpack items

Hero Traits

The Hero Traits are Power, Skill, and Wit. Every action you take within the world of *Scales & Tales* can be tested against these three Traits.

Your Hero Traits determine the personality of your character. Power is important to a Warrior but Wit might not be. And perhaps you have a Wizard that is not very strong or naturally charming but has studied very hard in school and therefore has a high Skill level and excels in spellcasting.

Everything you do playing *Scales & Tales* will be determined by rolling a twenty-sided die (d20) and adding it to your Hero Trait. You will be trying to get the highest possible number. If a player has low scores at first, that's okay! Character scores will increase as the quests progress.

Every obstacle or challenge in role-playing will have a Difficulty Level. Some Levels will be listed in the rule book, but as a GM, you will have to think quickly to determine a Difficulty Level when the situation comes up. See page 129 for more information about determining Difficulty Levels.

Power: Lifting, pounding, pulling, pushing, breaking, stamina, endurance, combat, allergies, resistance to poison, holding breath, withstanding pressure, willpower, hardiness

Skill: Shooting, balancing, acrobatics, sneaking, delicate moves, nimbleness, dodging, agility, reflexes, hand-eye coordination, language, book knowledge

Wit: Memory, reasoning, logic, focus, judge of character, intuition, common sense, street smarts, persuasion, bluffing, charm, influence, social magnetism, leadership

How to Use Your Hero Traits

Example 1:

The character Cybill is trying to pry open a sealed door. The door is rusted shut and has a secret Difficulty Level (DL) of 20. Cybill has a Power score of 11.

Cybill rolls a d20 and gets a 10.

Cybill's Power 11 + Roll 10 = 21 total

The 21 beats the door's DL20 rating.

Cybill takes a deep breath, uses all her strength, and successfully wrenches the door open.

Example 2:

In a dark hallway, the Hero Neem sees markings carved into the wall near a sealed door. Neem will roll for his Skill to see if he can read the language. Remembering a language is a skill you can learn. The secret Difficulty Level is 18.

Neem's Skill is an 11. He rolls a 4.

Neem's Skill of 11 + Roll 4 = 15 total

The 15 does not beat the DL18, so it looks like Neem was daydreaming in foreign languages that day.

Example 3:

A Dragonborn merchant tells the players to turn left, but Penny notices that the Dragonborn's eyes are darting back and forth and they seem very nervous. Penny wants to see if the Dragonborn is telling the truth. The secret Difficulty Level of the Dragonborn's lie is a 25.

Penny has a 12 for her Wit score. She rolls a 14. 12+14= 26. Penny's score of 26 beats the 25, so Penny senses that the Dragonborn is lying and signals to her party to go the other direction.

Experience Points (XP)

After the players roll for their Hero, they might notice that some of their Traits or HP are mediocre or even terrible. Don't worry! In between quests, Heroes can Level Up. Here's how it works:

During the quest, if the Hero does something that adds to the awesomeness of the game, the GM will award them with one or more Experience Points or XP. Here are some examples of things that may merit an Experience Point:

- being especially curious
- describing a really cool combat move
- saying your catchphrase at a really funny or opportune moment
- starting an inside joke
- being kind or helpful to the rest the players
- solving a puzzle
- encouraging teamwork

The GM will decide what merits XP on a moment-to-moment basis during the game.

Pro Tip: As a GM, you should give out lots of XP. It will keep your players excited and keep the pace of the game going quickly. Giving out XP encourages players to stay engaged and creative.

Leveling Up

A player can spend XP at any time of the quest to reroll one dice.

10 XP can be traded in between quests for the following Level Ups:

1. One at a time, the Hero rerolls the 3d6 dice for their Hero Traits. If the reroll is more than their current score, the Hero uses the new score. If the reroll is less than the current score, the Hero does nothing.

2. Permanently gain 1 HP.

3. Permanently gain one additional spot in the Hero's backpack.

Character Type

After determining your Hero Trait scores, you will choose your Character Type. All the Character Types are inherently equal, but each Type has specific, slightly different rules to emphasize their different strengths and weaknesses.

Human: The most opportunistic, malleable, and adaptable of all the Character Types.

Elf: An ancient and lofty creature, favoring grace and knowledge.

Dwarf: An ancient and hardy race, valuing craft and determination.

Ogre: A burly fantasy creature that is half civilized and half monstrous.

Goblin: A wild little troublemaker that is always extraordinary.

Werebeast: A meek human or a wild beast depending on the moon.

Frogling: A swamp creature that is somewhat frail but talented and amphibious.

Plantling: Actual animated plants that have chosen to be warriors. Wise but awkward.

Gnome: The tiniest character but sturdy and brimming with an old inherent magic.

Dragonborn: This ancient Type is the flashiest and most regal. Very skilled but frail; a glass hammer.

Choosing a Character Type

Heroes now determine their Character Type. Each character's description will instruct the Hero to immediately make changes to their Hero Trait scores. Heroes record this on their Character Sheets as they begin to develop their role-playing character. Players can select their perferred Type or roll a d20 to get a Type from the table below.

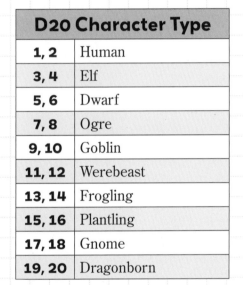

D20	Character Type
1, 2	Human
3, 4	Elf
5, 6	Dwarf
7, 8	Ogre
9, 10	Goblin
11, 12	Werebeast
13, 14	Frogling
15, 16	Plantling
17, 18	Gnome
19, 20	Dragonborn

Human

HP: 1d6 +3	Movement: 10 squares or 50 feet

In most role-playing games, the human represents the average character with the most common abilities. However, more than any other Character Type, humans tend to be adaptable and opportunistic. Perhaps in response to their average status in the fantasy world, humans are always desperately eager to prove themselves worthy.

Character Modifiers	Switch any two Hero Trait scores. Add 2 to any Hero Trait.
Stroke of Luck	Once per quest, reroll one dice any time.

Elf

HP: 1d6 +2	**Movement:** 12 squares or 60 feet

Elves are one of the most ancient and noble Types to live in the *Scales & Tales* world. Elves live in symbiosis with nature, have ornate architecture, and possess intricate combat skills. They have a nimble, cautious step and love their privacy. Elves can act like the wealthiest aristocrats or the most feral wildling.

Character Modifiers	Subtract 2 from Power. Add 2 to Skill.
Speed Burst	Once per quest, move 4 squares or 20 feet any time.

Dwarf

HP: 1d6 +4	**Movement:** 8 squares or 40 feet

Dwarves are a stoic, stern, and sturdy Character Type. Dwarves have a closed society and prefer to be isolated, protecting their wealth and complex mechanical infrastructures. Dwarves reside in deep mountain castles, thick forest enclaves, and weaving mining passageways. Dwarves greatly value friendship, family, and justice.

Character Modifiers	Subtract 3 from Wit. Add 2 to Skill and 1 to Power.
Picking Locks, Traps, and Mechanics	Roll 2d20 and choose the higher when dealing with machinery.

Ogre

HP: 1d6 +5	**Movement:** 10 squares or 50 feet

Ogres are brawny and burly creatures as old as the forests and mountains themselves. In fact, some say that the ogres were the very first warriors to descend from the wilderness. They are known to be somewhat dim, but they are the largest and strongest of the Character Types. Ogres can be brutish but can aspire to great heroism.

Character Modifiers	Add 3 to Power. Subtract 3 from Wit.
Infrared Vision	Ogres can see in the dark.
Hard Skin	Once per quest, the first time a ogre is dealt damage, reduce that damage to nothing.

Goblin

HP: 1d6 +1	**Movement:** 8 squares or 40 feet

Goblins are somewhat diminutive creatures that form complex societies in subterranean caverns and dark forest thickets. Even though they are sort of simple, they can excel in any skill and are renowned for their engineering feats. Goblins are easily overwhelmed and often excitable.

Character Modifiers	Goblins are *extra!* Add 4 to any one Trait and subtract 2 from the other two Traits.
Infrared Vision	Goblins can see in the dark.

Werebeast

HP: 1d6 as a human. 3d6 as a werebeast.	**Movement:** 10 squares or 50 feet

A werebeast changes from a normal-looking human to a beast-man in a matter of minutes. As a beast, the player is much stronger and nimbler, but its wild nature causes a lack of reason.

Character Modifiers	The player rolls a d6, called the Moondice, once every turn until they roll a 5 or 6. Then, the Hero adds 4 to Power and 2 to Skill, and subtracts 6 from Wit as the beast form. The beast form remains for five turns and then the Hero returns to human form and begins rolling the Moondice again.

Beast Table (Pick an animal)					
1	**2**	**3**	**4**	**5**	**6**
Goat	Rat	Wolf	Bear	Rabbit	Other

Frogling

HP: 1d6 +1	Movement: 8 squares or 40 feet

Froglings are mysterious creatures from the deep dark swamp. Froglings have soft, amphibious skin and are rather frail as adventurers, but they are virtually impossible to kill because they can regenerate their limbs. Froglings are also adept at any water task and have a mighty leap.

Character Modifiers	Subtract 4 from Power. Add 3 to Skill and 1 to Wit.
Water Advantage	Roll two d20 and choose the higher when dealing with water tasks.
Frog Leap	May leap 30 feet or 6 squares in any direction as an action.
Amphibious Regeneration	If a Frogling's HP would be 0, it becomes 1 instead.

Plantling

HP: 1d6	Movement: 10 squares or 50 feet

Plantlings are brave emissaries from the plant kingdom that have decided to become Heroes! Plantlings can take many different forms and don't always adhere to the rules of other creatures. Plantlings have an innate wisdom and calmness to them but sometimes act very awkward and out of place in the quickly-paced fantasy world of creatures and beasts.

Character Modifiers	Subtract 2 from Skill and add 1 to Wit and Power.
Regenerate	Plantlings regrow injured limbs and regain 1 point of HP each turn (not surpassing their starting HP).
Stoic	Plantlings can't panic or be scared.

Dice Table	
1	Vine
2	Houseplant
3	Cactus
4	Mushroom
5	Oak
6	Flower

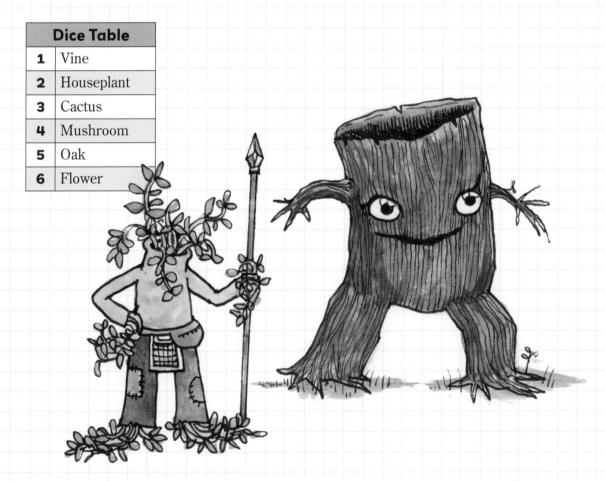

Gnome

HP: 1d6 +3	Movement: 10 squares or 50 feet

Gnomes are a tough, secretive, and magical Character Type. They reside in tiny tunnels, extremely remote villages, or forest hovels. They are the smallest of the Types and have a skin that resembles stone or leather. Gnomes possess a small amount of inherent magic within themselves and have been known to use that power in tricky and mischievous ways.

Character Modifiers	Subtract 3 from Power. Add 2 to Skill and 1 to Wit.
Telekinesis	The Hero can use their mind to move things ten pounds and under.

Dragonborn

HP: 1d6 +2	**Movement:** 12 squares or 60 feet

Dragonborn characters are the result of mixing human and dragon blood long ago. Their appearance can range from a scaled, reptilian beast on two legs to a creature of otherworldly beauty with a fiery disposition. Dragonborn possess a supernatural speed and strength but are a fragile and sickly Character Type.

Character Modifiers	Subtract 1 from Power. Add 3 to Skill.
Speed Burst	Once per quest, move 4 squares or 20 feet any time at all.

Hero Type

Each player will also need to choose a Hero Type. The players should look at their Hero Trait scores and begin to figure out what specialty might be good for their character.

Each Hero Type has its own advantages and drawbacks, and a balanced team will cover for each other's weaknesses.

With the other players, decide who will be which Hero Type, or test your luck by choosing randomly with a d20.

1–5 Guardian
The Guardian leads the group and leaves no friend behind.

6–10 Rogue
The Rogue operates with stealth, skill, and quick wit.

11–15 Wizard
The Wizard has the power of magic at their fingertips.

16–20 Warrior
The Warrior uses their heart and their muscles but also their brain and brawn.

Guardian

The Guardian is the most versatile Hero because they can do a bit of everything. They can heal other Heroes, they can cast some spells, and they are also well trained in combat. All these skills usually make the Guardian the leader of the party. Guardians are all about teamwork, cooperation, and justice.

Hero Skills

- Can hold a large weapon and use both hands
- Can choose one spell book to use
- As an action, heal any adjacent Hero by rolling 1d6 and adding that to their HP.
- Roll twice for Wit when Leveling Up and choose the higher one.

Example: Penny, the Goblin, makes a great leader. She excels at school, and she is the captain of the debate team. Some even call her "teacher's pet," though that isn't her favorite nickname. Penny's competitive nature makes her a powerful teammate, and her love for her pet rats shows she has the compassion necessary to be a good Guardian.

Rogue

SHHH

The Rogue is the wild card of the group, specializing in sneaking, ambushing, and other tricky tasks. They rely on careful planning and delicate maneuvers, and don't like heavy armor weighing them down and making lots of noise.

Hero Skills

- Delicate Advantage: Roll 2d20 and choose the greater for any Skill check.
- Sneak Attack: Add one dice if attacking the Enemy from the back.
- Roll twice for Skill when leveling up and choose the higher one.

Example: Cybill, the Elf, fits the role of Rogue very well. Except for math, she isn't really an ace at school because she prefers the nighttime hours and ends up snoozing in class. However, Cybill is fascinated by numbers and formulas and silently sneaks out of her house each night to make complex charts of the stars.

Warrior

Being a Warrior is all about attitude. It helps to be large and have brutish strength, but it's definitely not a requirement. Warriors love to fight and break things. They also value justice and bravery.

Hero Skills

- Can hold a two-handed weapon, or two one-handed weapons
- Blood Rage: If a Warrior inflicts damage on their first blow of combat, they immediately get one free attack.
- Warrior's Resilience: Once per quest, use an action to regain 1d6 HP.
- Roll twice for Power when Leveling Up.

Example: Porkchop, the Orc, is a born warrior. He was raised surfing and climbing trees on a tropical island where his family farmed coconuts and bananas. Surfing and lifting crates for years made Porkchop very strong and nimble. So much so that he was drafted for the national fistball team at a very young age. However, Porkchop's mother said that he has to graduate college before playing fistball and Porkchop agreed.

Wizard

The Wizard has the most knowledge of spellcasting in the group. The Wizard needs to use their spells and their brains because they aren't known to be very skilled in close combat.

Hero Skills
- Can choose three spell books to use
- Can only hold daggers, wands, staffs, and lanterns; can't wear metal armor
- Roll a 7 or above on a d20 at any time to detect evil.
- When leveling up, choose Skill or Wit. You may roll twice and choose the higher one.

Example: Neem the Wizard has large shoes to fill. He comes from a prestigious, rich family of Wizard elves and his parents have outfitted him with all the best equipment. Neem grew up in big castles and not in the real world, so he's a little clueless and has a lot of catching up to do in his social life.

    Neem is somewhat of a video game celebrity, winning multiple national championships and maintaining twelve thousand subscribed viewers on his weekly live feed, "Neem's World."

Personality Generator

Now that you know what Character Type and Hero Type your character is, it's time to develop your character's personality. Knowing a little bit more about your character's disposition and temperament will help you when role-playing. Work some of these traits and hobbies into the story during your quest. Roll twice if you want!

1	Prankster
2	Goth
3	Jock
4	Nerdy
5	Sneaky
6	Proud
7	Scheming
8	Hungry
9	Psychic
10	Artistic
11	Snazzy
12	Brave
13	Jumpy
14	Funny
15	Sarcastic
16	Gossipy
17	Loud
18	Sleepy
19	Lazy
20	Genius

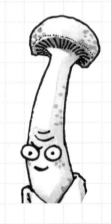

Hobbies and Interests

1	Activism
2	Reading
3	Nature
4	Cooking
5	Playing Music
6	Yoga
7	Bikes
8	Video Games
9	Sports
10	Thrifting
11	Crafting
12	Comics
13	Animals
14	Mechanics
15	Phone Freak
16	Dancing
17	Napping
18	Tree Houses
19	Board Games
20	Martial Arts

Backstory Generator

Creating a story about what happened to your Hero before the quest can go a long way in helping to understand your character and role-play better. Use the rolling tables to create a random backstory, or you can write your own.

Young Childhood	
1	Rich family
2	Poor family
3	Sickly child
4	Didn't speak for eight years
5	Loved to write
6	Loved to draw
7	Mean parents
8	Funny parents
9	Serious parents
10	Eighteen siblings
11	Only child
12	Adored animals
13	Idolized ninjas
14	Grew up on a farm
15	Grew up in a huge city
16	Known as a child genius
17	Ate really gross things for fun
18	Rode dirtbikes
19	Rode horses
20	Raised by penguins in the Antarctic

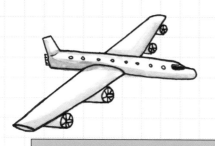

#	Hopes and Dreams	#	Turning Point
1	Marriage	1	Lost foot
2	Rich	2	Found money
3	Happy	3	Arrested
4	To be alone	4	Orphaned
5	Have a large family	5	Became a black belt in martial arts
6	Long for power	6	Separated by drought
7	Find a genie	7	Caught in a flood
8	Start a business	8	Chased away by monsters
9	Cure illness	9	Made an outcast
10	Overthrow government	10	Won lottery
11	Wanderlust	11	Moved far, far away
12	Compete in large tournaments	12	Found a wizard's book
13	Sports	13	Got a secret letter in the mail
14	Be a clown	14	Found a secret cave
15	Protect the land	15	Marooned on an island for a year
16	Protect people	16	Made an imaginary friend
17	Protect animals	17	Went to the future for 10 minutes
18	Travel a lot	18	Took a vow of silence
19	Become a commander	19	Started a business
20	Fame	20	Found an invisibility cloak

Fears	
1	Snakes
2	Water
3	Disloyalty
4	Violence
5	Magic
6	Dragons
7	Small talk
8	Untidiness
9	Heights
10	Fire
11	Germs
12	The dark
13	Blood
14	Bathing
15	Crowds
16	Tombs/Graveyards
17	Boredom
18	Mirrors
19	Being laughed at
20	Loud Noise

Weapons and Gear

Use this section to choose the weapons, armor, and gear that your Heroes will bring with them on their quest. Each Type of Hero can only hold, carry, and wear a certain number of weapons and items. Some of the items have no description on purpose so that the players can use their imaginations to create the abilities and descriptions of the items. Have fun!

Hero Type	What Can They Hold?	Backpack Capacity	What Can They Wear?
Guardian	Any 2 items	3 items (Guardian already carries a spell book)	Metal, leather, cloth
Rogue	1 weapon, 1 item	4 items	Leather, cloth, organic
Wizard	1 weapon, 1 item	1 item (Wizard has 3 spell books already)	Leather, cloth, organic
Warrior	Any 2 items or two-handed weapon	4 items	Metal, leather, cloth

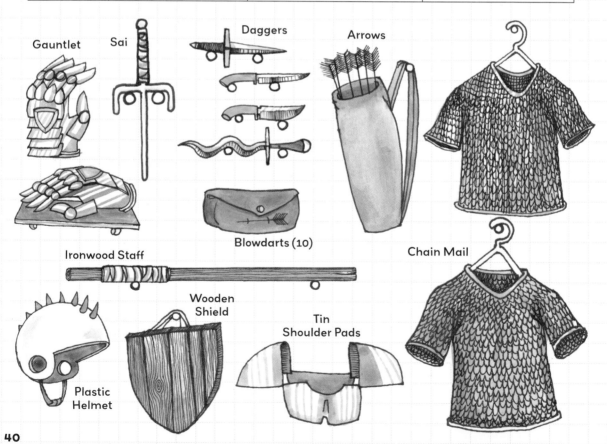

Gauntlet

Sai

Daggers

Arrows

Blowdarts (10)

Chain Mail

Ironwood Staff

Wooden Shield

Tin Shoulder Pads

Plastic Helmet

Weapon	Attack Dice	Defense Dice	Range
Two-Handed Axe	4	0	Adjacent
Two-Handed Warhammer	4	0	Adjacent
Two-Handed Sword	3	1	Close
Spiked Mace	3	0	Adjacent
Broadsword	2	1	Adjacent
Rapier	2	1	Adjacent
Oak Bow and Arrows	2	0	12 squares or 60 ft
Whip	1	0	Close
Sai	1	1	Adjacent

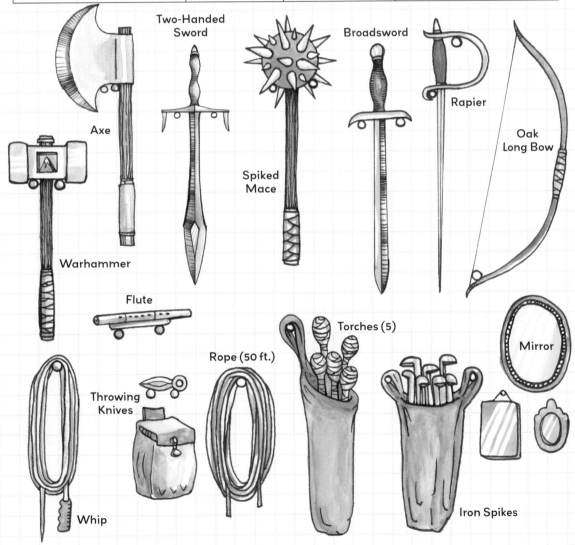

Weapon	Attack Dice	Defense Dice	Range
Ironwood Staff	1	1	Close
Blowdart	1	0	10 squares or 50 ft
Throwing Knife	1	0	8 squares or 40 ft
Gauntlet	1	2	Adjacent
Dagger	2	0	Adjacent
Plastic Helmet	0	1	Armor
Wooden Shield	0	2	Armor
Tin Shoulder Pads*	0	3	Armor *counts as 2 items
Metal Chain Mail	0	1	Armor
Leathers	0	1	Armor

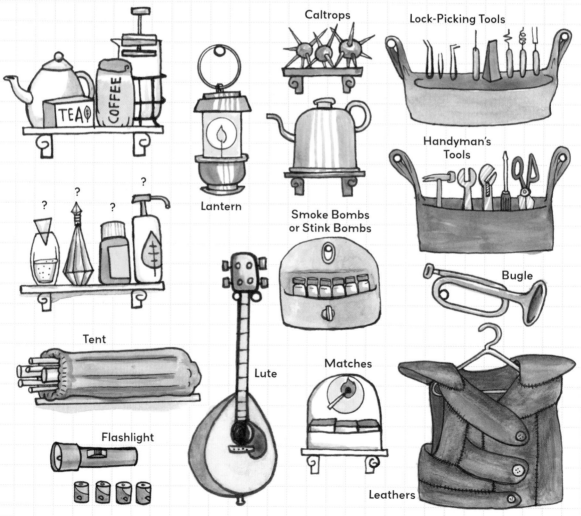

Caltrops

Lock-Picking Tools

Handyman's Tools

?   ?   ?   ?

Lantern

Smoke Bombs or Stink Bombs

Bugle

Tent

Lute

Matches

Flashlight

Leathers

Range

Range is how far a weapon can reach on the game board. In *Scales & Tales*, range is determined by three distances: adjacent, close, and far. A weapon or spell with a far range will list how far that weapon can reach.

Adjacent means the four squares right next to the Heroes. Most one- and two-handed weapons need to be adjacent to strike; that is, within five feet.

Close means the squares diagonal from the Hero and one square away. Staffs, whips, spears, chains, and other weapons are able to attack close targets; that is, within seven to ten feet.

Far means anything that the Hero can see in their line of sight. Every ranged weapon will have a distance listed with the weapon. Everything within that range is an easy shot and the Hero can just roll their attack dice. If the distance is greater than the weapon's range, the Hero must test their Skill with a d20 and a Difficulty Level determined by the GM.

FFTTT

Spellcasting

Heroes can cast magical spells during their turn as an action. Wizards and Guardians start the game with spells at their disposal in the form of spell books.

The Wizard chooses three spell books and the Guardian chooses one spell book. At the start of the game, the Wizard chooses the first spell book, the Guardian chooses the second spell book, and then the Wizard chooses their other two spell books. Heroes can't choose a spell book more than once.

To cast a spell: On their turn, the Hero declares what spell they are casting, and the spell is cast as written. The GM will decide how it affects the gameboard and the story of the game. Succeed or fail, the spell scroll then crumbles in the Hero's hand unless stopped by a special ability.

Game Master Tip: Remind your spellcasters that they don't need to save up their spells and can use them freely, since they will be regenerated each night.

Wizard

The Wizard carries three spell books. After casting a spell, the Wizard may test their Skill or Wit score against the DL of 20. If they succeed, they may keep their spell.

Guardian

The Guardian carries one spell book. After casting a spell, the Guardian may test their Skill or Wit score agaist the DL of 20. If they succeed, they may keep their spell.

The Seven Spell Books

Book of Air

Gust of Speed	Double your Movement for one round.
Whirlwind Cyclone 	Target Enemy loses its next turn and moves 1d6 spaces away.
Flying	+2 Movement Squares, move over Enemies and terrain, ground Enemies' attacks reduced by 1d6, ends when Hero is dealt 1 point of damage.

Book of Water

Washing Wave	Summon a wave 2d6 wide, all creatures in wave lose their following turn.
Water of Life	Add 2d6 HP to any one Hero.
Conjure Elemental	Summon 1d6 loyal Water Sprites with: 1 Attack Dice, 1 Defense Dice, 1 HP. If water is nearby, summon 3d6 Sprites.

Book of Fire

Firestorm	All Enemies in a four-square radius (40 ft radius) take 1 HP damage.
Red-Eyed Rage	All Heroes gain two Attack Dice for 1d6 turns.
Bolt of Lightning 	Choose one Enemy you can see. Deal 2 HP damage to that creature.

Book of the Earth

Thick Hide	Target Hero gains 3 Defense Dice for 1d6 turns.
Chasm	Starting from the spellcaster, a chasm in the ground opens 1 square (5 ft) wide and 1d20 long. All monsters in the path disappear and Enemies can no longer cross the chasm.
Earth Force	Target Hero gains 2d6 HP.

Book of the Heart

Devoted Friendship	Target Enemy now follows the Hero's every command, even combat.
Telekinesis	Telepathically move one item, equal to or less than the Hero's weight.
Delicious Meal	Time stops and a banquet of food and drink appears before the Heroes. All Heroes gain 1d6 HP and gain advantage on the next dice roll.

Book of the Dark

Sleep	1d6 number of Enemies are rendered helpless for two rounds.
Fear	Enemies each lose 2 Attack Dice for 1d6 rounds.
Crumble	Target item made of wood, metal, or stone cracks and crumbles apart, making it useless.

Book of the Weird

Genie	Choose up to three of the following abilities. The genie disappears after the third wish: Deal 1 damage, detect traps, disarm traps, open a door, fly one turn, disappear one turn, heal 1d6 HP, target Enemy loses one turn, counter target Enemy spell.
Teleport	Move unseen and unhurt to any space you can see or have been.
Transmute	Change any one thing into anything else of the same size and mass, per the GM's approval.

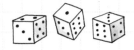 

Combat

*Scales & Tale*s uses a fun and easy method of fantasy combat utilizing six-sided dice. The number of d6 that you roll is determined by the weapons and armor you hold and wear.

Certain spells, artifacts, and advantages will boost or reduce the amount of Attack or Defense Dice the Hero can roll.

When a Hero is standing adjacent or within range of an Enemy, they may roll their Attack Dice.

Attacking

Every roll of a 4, 5, or 6 is 1 HP of damage to the Enemy. The Enemy can roll its Defense Dice to reduce this number, but every undefended roll subtracts 1 HP of damage from the Enemy.

Defending

When a Hero is attacked, they roll with their Defense Dice to try to reduce that damage. Every Hero starts with one Defense Dice, just for wearing clothes and being alive. Every roll of 5 or 6 reduces the damage taken by one.

 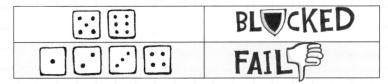

Evil Defense

In *Scales & Tale*s, evil forces have a disadvantage when defending since being evil leads to a certain carelessness. Enemies only successfully defend on a roll of 6.

Example of Combat

Porkchop is battling a Brambling and a Weirdling. It may help to act this scenario out with players so they can get an idea of how combat works.

Porkchop		
Attack	Defense	HP
3	2	10

Brambling		
Attack	Defense	HP
2	1	1

Weirdling		
Attack	Defense	HP
1	1	1

Porkchop swings first and rolls a 4, 3, and 2. So one of their hits land on the Brambling, the 4.

However, the Brambling rolls a 6 and defends successfully.

Then the Brambling attacks and rolls a 5 and a 3. Porkchop rolls a 2 and a 6 and successfully defends.

The Weirdling attacks but rolls a 3, so damage is inflicted. A swing and a miss!

Porkchop swings his axe and rolls a 5, 6, and 1. Two hits to the Brambling. The Brambling rolls a 2 in defense, but nothing could have saved the little dude this time. The Brambling explodes in a leafy puff.

Porkchop is energized! He is a Warrior, so the rules say he gets another attack! He rolls a 1, 4, and 3. The remaining Weirdling rolls a pitiful 3 and is vaporized by Porkchop's axe.

Enemies

Some Enemies are so big that before you can roll your combat dice, you must pass a Power test. A lower-level tricky beast might require a combined Power and d20 roll of 15. For a supremely evil Bad Boss, a player may need to equal a 20, 25, or higher Difficulty Level.

Weirdling

Attack Dice	Defense Dice	HP	Movement
1	1	1	4 squares or 20 feet

The smallest minion of the evil forces, these little dudes barely stand taller than your knee, but many of them together can be overwhelming.

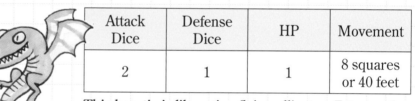

Zat

Attack Dice	Defense Dice	HP	Movement
2	1	1	8 squares or 40 feet

This beastie is like a tiny flying alligator. Zats can fly over terrain and Heroes. These feral pests have a dangerous SNAP!

Brambling

Attack Dice	Defense Dice	HP	Movement
2	1	1	5 squares or 25 feet

Evil has found the body of foliage. These angry goons are like animated malevolent shrubs.

Zibble

Attack Dice	Defense Dice	HP	Movement
2	2	1	8 squares or 40 feet

These Enemies are hippy, angry, little four-legged goobers. They act like a snappy basketball with shark teeth.

Scorpy

Attack Dice	Defense Dice	HP	Movement
2	3	2	6 squares or 30 feet

These tiny insectoid troops with bumbling discipline have a "sleepy sting." If a Scorpy does damage to a Hero, the Hero must roll a d20 and add it to their Power score. If that combined number isn't 20 or more, that Hero loses their next turn.

Gritch

Attack Dice	Defense Dice	HP	Movement
3	2	2	6 squares or 30 feet

You might think these are evil gibbering shadows, but these capable warriors are like angry burnt trees with sharp, crooked swords.

Gremlin

Attack Dice	Defense Dice	HP	Movement
3	4	2	10 squares or 50 feet

These Enemies can be compared to barking bazooka bulldogs. Gremlins are shadowy beasts filled with a mindless evil and are very dangerous.

Bork

Attack Dice	Defense Dice	HP	Movement
2	2	2	8 squares or 40 feet

These Enemies are ferocious and calculating hogs that roam the rugged countryside and are sometimes kept as guard hogs by Trolls.

Reptoid

Attack Dice	Defense Dice	HP	Movement
3	3	2	8 squares or 40 feet

Reptoids are corrupted dark warriors with the bodies of fierce skittering lizards. They're obedient and regimented troops but are easily fooled.

Troll

Attack Dice	Defense Dice	HP	Movement
4	3	3	8 squares or 40 feet

A giant, strong, cruel, evil bruiser with a love of money and a taste for flesh. Diabolically, intelligently evil and mean-tempered.

Persuasion

Combat isn't the only way to interact with an enemy! If you don't want a battle on your hands, roll a d20 and add the result to your Wit score. If you score 20 or over, use one of the following persuasion methods and avoid a fight!

Flattery: Give your enemy a compliment! Almost everyone loves to hear good things about themselves, even if they aren't true!

Lying: Flat-out fibbing. Most people try to lie, but not many are very convincing. Make it believable and it might throw your enemy off.

Distraction: Change the subject! What was that sound over there? Distraction could be anything from a wild outfit to a phantom rustle in the woods.

Meekness: Convince the baddies that they're so much more powerful than you, it would be worthless to even try.

Arguing: You know you're right and you're gonna let everyone know! Make sure you bring all your evidence and receipts, because you don't want to lose this argument!

TIME TO PLAY!

At this point, players have filled out their Character Sheet and created their characters. Now they can start to role-play! Heroes take turns moving around the game environment and taking actions. To decide the order of turns, each player rolls a d20 and the players play from highest result to lowest.

A game that you can complete in one session is called a **quest.**

A bunch of quests that make up a larger story is called a **campaign.**

Scales & Tales is both a set of rules for beginning players and a sample campaign, titled:

TOAD ISLAND.

Combat is a fun and traditional part of role-playing, but sometimes fighting Enemies all day gets boring. The Toad Island campaign is meant to demonstrate how a GM can incorporate mini games, party puzzles, and drawing games into role-playing stories.

The following is the Toad Island campaign. The entire campaign is composed of quests that should take two or three hours each. As the quests progress along the campaign, players accumulate better items, and their characters get more developed. Remind players to write down everything that happens to their character and everything they might collect on their Character Sheets.

Toad Island   Backstory

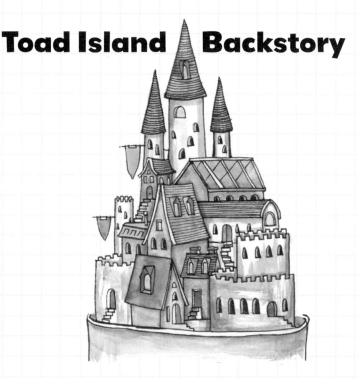

A backstory is very important to role-playing because it helps explain the motivation of your Heroes and allows everyone to start their imaginations in the same place. The GM should read this part aloud before the Toad Island campaign:

It was a normal day in the great hall at Sherrywood Forest, Institute for Heroes. Young orcs and humans were sparring with training swords. A group including gnomes, dwarves, and a spotted frogling were tinkering with a little robot.

A giggling goblin and a few happy halflings were avoiding their chemistry homework by mixing up a rancid fart bomb. A luminescent young elf and a scaled Dragonborn both combed their hair with ornate magical combs. Every Character Type was treated equally at Sherrywood Institute, and it was because of this policy that the school produced the most well-rounded Heroes and champions.

Striding between her pupils was the stunning and terrifying headmaster, WynWyn Gral. She was a well-known world adventurer, with many tales of her epic quests circulating the land. It was said that she saved the world many times, and she now transferred that same zeal into being a devoted educator. She knew the next generation of Heroes was the world's best hope for the future.

Whether the students loved WynWyn or feared her stern attitude, every single soul in the school respected her and sought her approval.

Suddenly, the ambient chatter of the school was shattered as a monstrous figure crashed through the wall of the great hall. It was Edwin Tortice, a well-known Warrior and Lord of Toad Island. Edwin had been known to be a great and benevolent leader, but now it seemed that evil had twisted and mutated his body to enormous proportions.

Edwin's giant sword sliced through the stone walls like they were cake. Tossing aside bookshelves and students, Edwin took a few giant steps across the room.

Edwin was after Tazzaphur, the moon drake, a magical little dragon who was the beloved mascot of the school. Tazzaphur the mascot was playful and silly, and every student loved "Tazz."

The moon drake was a very rare beast, the only one on the planet, and was known to possess a great amount of magic. However, Edwin's whole body was pulsating with an evil energy, and he was able to snatch Tazz right out of the sky. The moon drake let out a terrified shriek as Edwin grabbed it around its scaly neck.

Just then, WynWyn used her telekinesis to shift the furniture loudly and deliberately in the room to free the students caught under the rubble and to get Edwin's attention. She was not about to let this happen in her school, and Edwin was going to know it.

"Don't dare follow me!" bellowed Edwin, as he took another monster swipe at the castle wall with his huge sword. Giant pieces of rubble crumbled down in the great hall as students desperately tried to get out of the way of the debris.

Scowling blankly, Edwin set fire to a bookshelf full of magical tomes.

WynWyn quickly darted across the room, selflessly rescuing many students as she went. Fire and stone rained down around her as she used her magic and brute strength to lift young elves and halflings from the chaos. She took a lot of damage but managed to get everyone out of harm's way.

By the time WynWyn had rescued the last student, Edwin Tortice was long gone. He'd escaped with Tazzaphur, the moon drake, and was no doubt on his way back to his mountain stronghold.

Tendrils of smoke waft from the wreckage of the Institute. WynWyn calls your group over to her. Charred and spent, she says, "Edwin Tortice is the Lord of Toad Island. He will be in his castle stronghold. You must follow him. You are my best students and the best hope for our school. Find out what has turned Edwin Tortice into this monster."

"And you must find and rescue Tazzaphur, our beloved mascot . . . he must be so scared . . ."

Toad Island Campaign

1. **The Bully**

   The Heroes must confront the school bully while pursuing their foe.

2. **Escape from Heroes' Institute**

   Rescue the map of Turtle Island and get out of the chaotic school alive.

3. **The Road to Turtle Island**

   Encounter some wild monsters and learn how you can tame magical Familiars.

4. **The Hydra**

   Encounter a gigantic, tricky dragon.

5. **Troll Castle**

   The Heroes raid the castle of some greedy trolls in a dark forest.

6. **River Crossing**

   Cross a raging river in a tiny boat as it is harangued by strange river monsters and pesky pirates.

7. Rescue Sniffkin

In the port town of Turtle Island, the Heroes must rescue a kidnapped child from an evil boss.

8. Jailbreak at Castle Gorgox

Free the innocent citizens that the Gorgox has locked in his castle dungeon.

9. Deadly Dash

The angry Gorgox chases the Heroes down! They must escape through the woods!

10. Airship

All aboard the airship to take the Heroes to Tortice Heights while watching out for flying Enemies.

11. Gallopi Gus

The first of the two mystics, Gus, will challenge the Heroes with a riddle to obtain his assistance.

12. Byron Blink

Another mystic poses a challenge that the Heroes must complete in order to receive a powerful artifact.

13. Castle Tortice

Battle through the final castle and fight the big boss.

14. The Battle of Turtle Island

More surprises await the Heroes atop Turtle Island. An incredibly powerful hidden danger is revealed and an old ally returns.

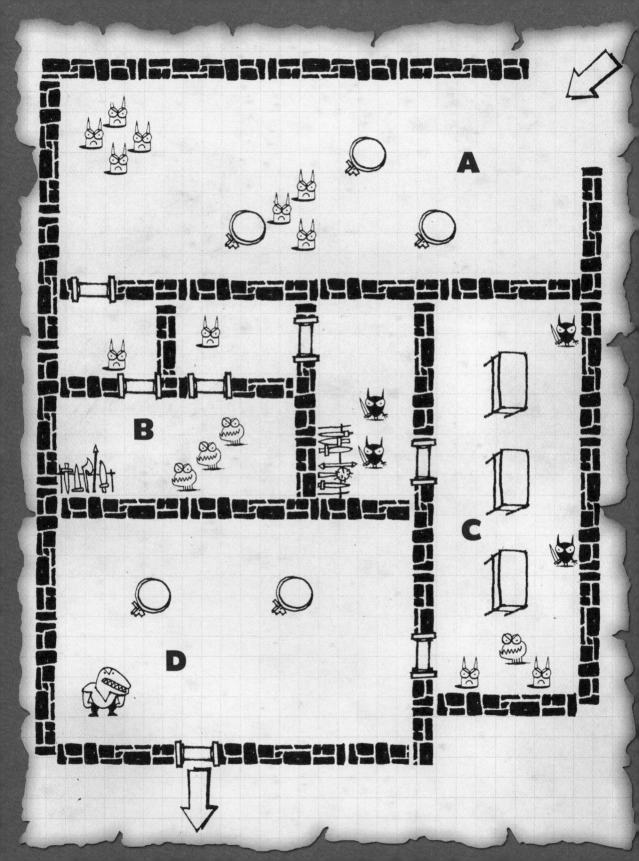

The Bully

Edwin Tortice has just demolished the Heroes' school and injured the headmaster! They must avenge these wrongs and rescue their beloved school mascot, Tazz! But first, they must get out of the school itself!

A. Heroes start in the Main Hall right after Edwin flees. Wynwyn is there, but her leg is badly injured and she can't go with them. She reminds the Heroes that there are a few good teacher's weapons hidden throughout the school.

B. If the Heroes search for secrets in this room, they will find a crossbow (3 Attack Dice, 14 squares range, 70ft.).

C. If the Heroes search the hallways for secrets, they will find a lever beneath a painting on the wall. It clicks open a secret room containing a Cool Wizard Staff (two handed, 2 Attack Dice, 1 Defense Dice). When found, roll for a spell on the Scroll Table. The Staff holds the spell, and the Hero can cast that spell once per quest.

D. Outside the library stands Daylor Penth, high elf debutant, bully of the school, and end boss of the quest. Daylor's favorite thing in the world is to bully and demean those around him. You will have to beat him at his own game. It's very important for this game to keep the insults clean and without curses while making them as insulting as possible.

Cave-dwelling, purple-bellied, salt-stumped, fluff-tailed, snub-nosed, fish-tongued, nonrenewable, greasy-haired, green-gilled, glop-headed, half-perished, flabby-headed, cod-faced, sea-drinking, shark-eyed, overblown, insect-eyed, puddle-dwelling	Pompous, stinky, selfish, feathered, scales, smelly, crusty, crumbly, dead-eyed, soggy, knobby, slimy, drippy, boneless, genetically modified, festering, frosty, sour, blundering	Buzzard, donkey, skunk, weevil, stain, smear, blob, snot bag, mud pudding, muck brain, sludge face, fool, contagious rash, armpit stain, dirty boot, cuddler, sniffer, bucket

When the players each create their own insult NOT based on the chart, you can declare them the winner. Good insults get XP. Each player rolls for treasure and scrolls.

"CLICK!"

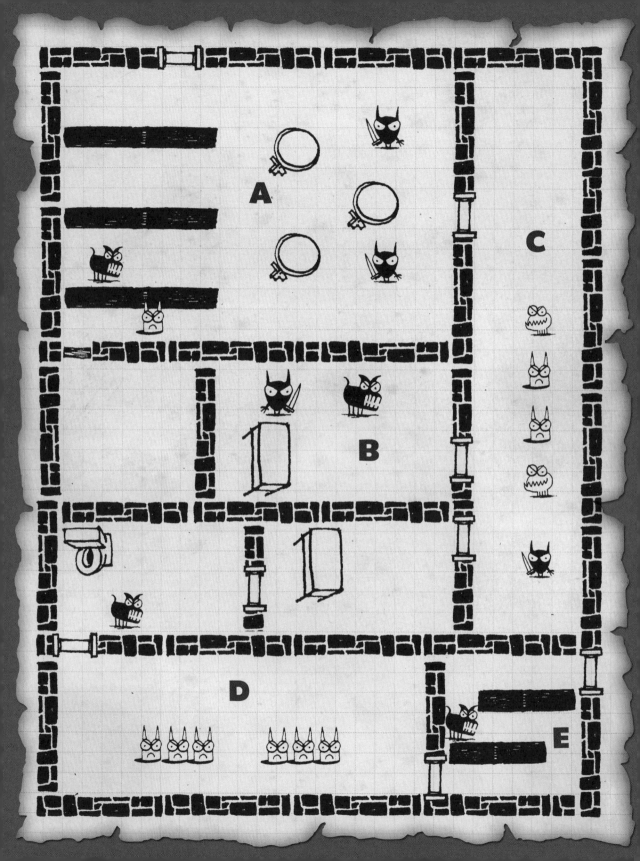

Escape from Heroes' Institute

Your characters have found themselves in the library of Sherrywood Forest, Institute for Heroes. Now, the Heroes must obtain the Map to Turtle Island and escape the school.

A. This is the library. A simple search will show that the Map to Toad Island is in a flat, clear display case up on the wall. However, the clear case is protected with a powerful magic and nothing the Heroes can do will break or open the case.

    If the Heroes search for secrets, tell them that WynWyn has set a simple verification test on the case that can only be opened if the Heroes describe their favorite book. The book should be one that the character would like. Once each Hero describes their perfect book, the case pops open.

B. If the Heroes search for secrets, they find a small Metal Shield in the teacher's desk.

0 Attack Dice	2 Defense Dice

C. This is the science room, filled with bunsen burners and anatomy posters. Each player must describe and draw what their character would present in a science fair. Players all get XP, and the best project gets a spell scroll.

D. The Heroes enter the gym and see that they've interrupted a game of dodgeball between weirdlings, and now they're all in hot pursuit of the Heroes!

E. This room is filled with racks of sports balls, but there are Zibbles hidden among them! If the Heroes don't search for secrets, the Zibbles jump out and surprise them!

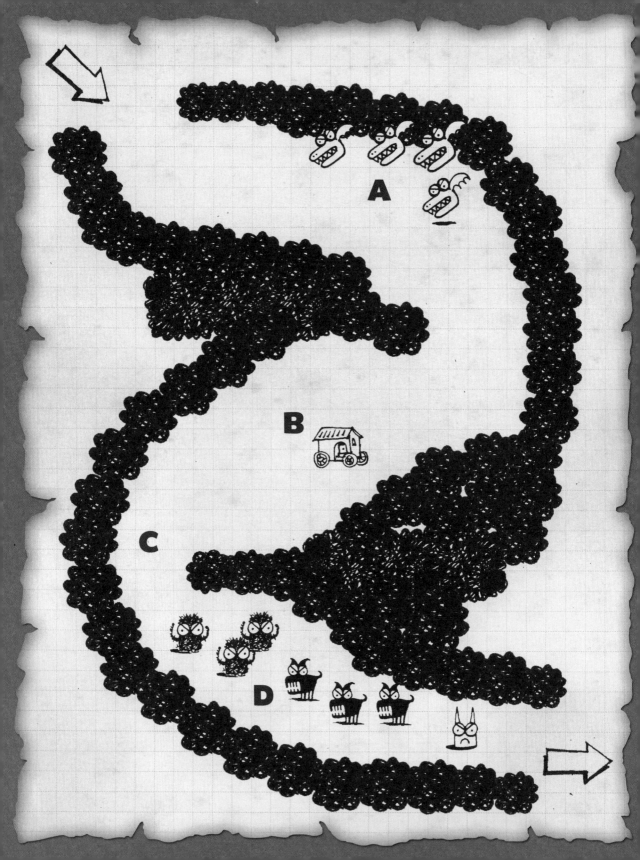

A

B

C

D

The Road to Toad Island

Toad Island is a far journey from the Heroes' Institute. The Heroes will find both friend and foe on their mission there.

A. Zats are flying creatures and have slightly different rules: 1. If a Hero is attacking with a hand weapon, reduce Attack Dice by 1. Staffs, two-handed weapons, and ranged weapons work normally.

B. For the Heroes: Here on the road, you come across a bright, kind Dragonborn dressed in a three-piece suit and top hat. He introduces himself with a slight accent as Lars Depple and acts kind and humble. A cute little bat nuzzles his armpit and a stoat twirls around Lars's hat. His rickety carriage is stuck in a small mud puddle. Pulling the carriage with apparent difficulty is his unidonkey, Hank Saturday. Hank is acting tired and frustrated. Once or twice when Hank exerts himself, you see him fart a tiny rainbow cloud.

Lars's carriage is a small sleeper carriage, piled high with all sorts of tinctures, potions, bottles, feathers, dreamcatchers, crystals, stones, books, and scrolls.

GM: Any search for secrets will tell you he seems harmless. Lars will trade with the Heroes two or three items found on the treasure or spell scroll lists.

When the Heroes offer to help Lars out of the mud, turn to the next page.

C. Each player should have the opportunity to attract at least one Familiar.

D. This quest ends in a drama: The group can see Lars and his carriage down the road. The group of Heroes watch in horror as a group of three huge trolls bully and shove Lars and his unidonkey. They steal a number of items from Lars and head into the dark forest.

A Magician & His Familiars

MAJOR PLOT POINT: If the Heroes try to help Lars out of the puddle, he will deny the help, and tell you he wants to show you something. He takes out a small pad of paper and carefully draws something on the pad and then shows it to them. Suddenly, the Heroes feel a warm wind, and they see an armadillo appear from the woods. The armadillo helps push the carriage from behind, and the carriage rolls out of the mud.

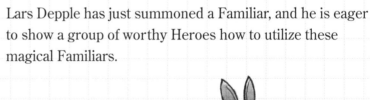

Lars Depple has just summoned a Familiar, and he is eager to show a group of worthy Heroes how to utilize these magical Familiars.

Summoning Familiars

Familiars are little forest animal friends that help Heroes along their quests.

A Hero may choose Summon a Familiar as their action for the turn.

In *Scales & Tales,* you play a drawing game to summon a Familiar.

1. The Hero rolls a d6. This roll will determine which drawing table to use. The Hero then rolls a d20. This roll will determine the secret clue.

2. The GM will whisper the clue or write it down on a secret slip of paper and show it to the Hero. The Hero has five seconds to think, and then one minute to draw the clue without speaking.

3. If the other Heroes successfully guess the clue, the winning Hero rolls another d20 to determine the Familiar that the Hero has summoned. If the other Heroes do not guess your drawing, your turn is over.

4. The winning Hero can now follow the rules on the card until the Familiar is A. returned to the wild or B. traded out.

Drawing Tables

1	2	3	4	5	6
Easy	Verb	Nouns	Adjectives	Wild Card	Difficult

1. Easy

1	Pegasus
2	Ship
3	Tadpole
4	Thorn
5	Pelican
6	Trombone
7	Spider
8	Feather
9	Rain
10	Catfish
11	River
12	Den
13	Rattlesnake
14	Butterfly
15	Shield
16	Ghost
17	Pizza
18	Smoke
19	Cactus
20	Duck

2. Verb

1	Fill
2	Flow
3	Snore
4	Overturn
5	Occupy
6	Split
7	Shave
8	Sprain
9	Stumble
10	Hunt
11	Swim
12	Pick
13	Flip
14	Wink
15	Think
16	Twist
17	Pat
18	Exercise
19	Pose
20	Tunnel

3. Nouns

1	Omelet
2	Stomach
3	Steak
4	Frosting
5	Island
6	Skillet
7	Dad
8	Totem Pole
9	Toast
10	Leak
11	Voice
12	Safe
13	Jury
14	Headache
15	Surgery
16	Picnic
17	Universe
18	Blizzard
19	Idea
20	Lunch

4. Adjectives	
1	Skinny
2	Rich
3	Handsome
4	Late
5	Messy
6	Sharp
7	Wet
8	Dark
9	Smart
10	Injured
11	Enraged
12	Lazy
13	Quick
14	Moody
15	Dry
16	Slippery
17	Secret
18	Clear
19	Far
20	Valuable

5. Wildcard	
1	Ponder
2	Drape
3	Align
4	Darkroom
5	Hurricane
6	Pivot
7	Laundry
8	Poison
9	Tune
10	Cough
11	Mirage
12	Fever
13	Lawn
14	Cook
15	Scuff
16	Glance
17	Ripple
18	Magnet
19	Diagram
20	Grow

Mystic 6. Difficult	
1	Language
2	Whole
3	Near
4	Upside Down
5	Paper
6	Poem
7	Rust
8	Midnight
9	Translator
10	Story
11	Lame
12	Scenery
13	Word
14	Slow Motion
15	Fear
16	Guess
17	Caffeine
18	Dense
19	Reflect
20	Habit

Make your own! There are blank d20 tables in the back of this book, so fill in your own secret clue table when you get tired of these clues.

About Familiars

Record the information about your Familiars on the back of your Character Sheet.

Static Ability: When a Hero has possession of a Familiar, that Hero always has the ability listed on the card. These will usually affect the Hero Trait numbers or movement numbers.

Penguin

+2 Movement Squares	+1 Skill

RW: Action Surge, immediately take another action

You may keep up to three small Familiars. Small Familiars are 1–9 on the d20 Familiars table.

You may keep one medium and one small Familiar. Medium Familiars are 10–20 on the d20 Familiars table.

You may only have one Mystic Familiar and nothing else.

Only if you roll a 6 for the difficult drawing table and are successful, may you roll for a Mystic Familiar.

Return to the **W**ild (**RW**): When the Hero uses this ability, they won't have this Familiar anymore. The animal has used its greatest ability and it returns to nature. The Hero discards their Familiar card or notes the returned creature on the back of their Character Sheet. RW can be used instantly during anyone's turn.

Table of Familiars

1	chipmunk
2	toad
3	cat
4	otter
5	parrot
6	bat
7	rabbit
8	salamander
9	hummingbird
10	fox
11	owl
12	penguin
13	crow
14	javelina
15	skunk
16	snapping turtle
17	monkey
18	eagle
19	armadillo
20	raccoon

small (1–9)

medium (10–20)

Mystic Familiars

If a Hero draws a difficult clue and the rest of the party guesses it correctly, they roll a d20 to choose a Mystic Familiar.

1-5	**6-10**	**11-15**	**16-20**
Jackalope	Ivory Sphinx	Onyx Pugera	Jade Griffix

Chipmunk

+1 Skill

RW: Reroll one dice

Toad

+1 Power

RW: Roll with an additional Defense Dice in combat

Cat

+1 Wit

RW: Roll with two dice and choose the better one

Otter

+1 Power

RW: Roll with an additional Attack Dice in combat

Parrot

+1 Wit

RW: Target Enemy is frozen in place for one round

Bat

+1 Wit

RW: Any damage done to target Enemy this turn is lethal

Rabbit

+3 Movement Squares

RW: Move 3 squares any time at all

Salamander

+2 Power

RW: Gain 2 HP

Hummingbird

+2 Wit

RW: Gain flying for 1d6 turns (+2 movement squares or 10 ft, move over Enemies and terrain, ground Enemies' attacks reduced by one dice)

Fox

+2 Skill	+1 Attack Dice

RW: Hero gets two attacks this turn

Owl

+2 Skill

RW: Counter target Enemy spell

Penguin

+2 movement squares	+1 Skill

RW: Action Surge, immediately take another action

Crow

+2 Skill

RW: Automatically succeed on one Wit check

Javelina

+1 Defense Dice	+1 Power

RW: Add 2 Defense Dice to your next defensive roll

Skunk

+2 Wit	Enemies lose 1 Defense Dice

RW: Creatures in a 4 square radius of Hero are stunned for one full round

Snapping Turtle

+3 Power

RW: Action Surge, immediately take another action

Monkey

+2 Skill	All traps are visible

RW: Action Surge, immediately take another action

Eagle

+2 squares on ranged attacks	+2 Wit

RW: Do 2 HP damage to any target you can see

Armadillo

+2 Power	+2 Defense Dice

RW: You cannot take damage this round

Raccoon

+2 Skill	+2 Wit

RW: Remotely pick one lock or open a door or disarm a trap

Mystic
Jackalope

+6 movement squares	+2 Skill

RW: Move 6 squares any time at all

Mystic
Ivory Sphinx

For every point of damage you deal, you gain that much life

RW: Gain 8 HP

Mystic
Onyx Pugera

+2 Attack Dice

RW: Deal 1 HP damage to all creatures within a 9 square radius OR deal 3 HP damage to one target

Mystic
Jade Griffix

Move unrestricted through doors, walls, terrain, and Enemies

RW: Teleport up to 12 squares or to any place you have already been this quest

Hydra's Lair

Along the road, the Heroes will find Enemies small and very big! A giant, dragon-headed Hydra stalks the woods. It has the body of a triceratops and has six snarling heads at the end of six long snake-like necks. Slaying this hydra will require more than just swinging a sword.

When the Heroes reach this point, they can see the Hydra. Use the rules on the following pages to battle the Hydra.

After the Hydra is defeated, each Hero receives one item from the treasure table and one item from the scroll table.

Six-Headed Hydra

The Hydra has six attacks per turn. During the Hydra's turn, it will target a Hero and attack with one: Snapping Jaw (2 Attack Dice) and the Hero can defend as normal. It will choose another nearby target and repeat this five times. The Hydra will target the same Hero more than once if no other Hero is close.

Each Hero immediately gets a counterattack, but only if they defeat a difficulty level of 20 using their Power or Skill.

If the player's roll and the Hero Trait score is 20 or above, the Hero may attack using their Attack Dice as normal. If the Hero can deal 1 HP damage to the head, the head is SEVERED. The Hero rolls a d6 to determine what grows from the severed stump. The players should record the heads of the Hydra by drawing them. A Hydra template has been provided.

1	2	3	4	5	6
Another Head	Hand	Foot	Tail	Horn	Giant Finger

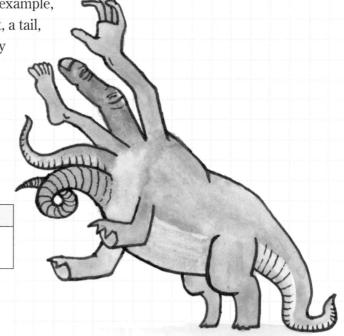

While the Hydra has ANY heads, the Hydra will only attack with its heads. For example, if the Hydra has three heads, a foot, a tail, and a finger left, the Hydra can only attack three times during its turn.

The Heroes must fight the Hydra until all the heads are cut off. At that point, the MIXED-UP HYDRA only gets one attack and combat may operate normally.

Mixed-Up Hydra		
6 Attack Dice	2 Defense Dice	4 HP

Hydra Template

Use the Hydra template on this page to help you draw, but remember to use pencil, because the heads may switch around!

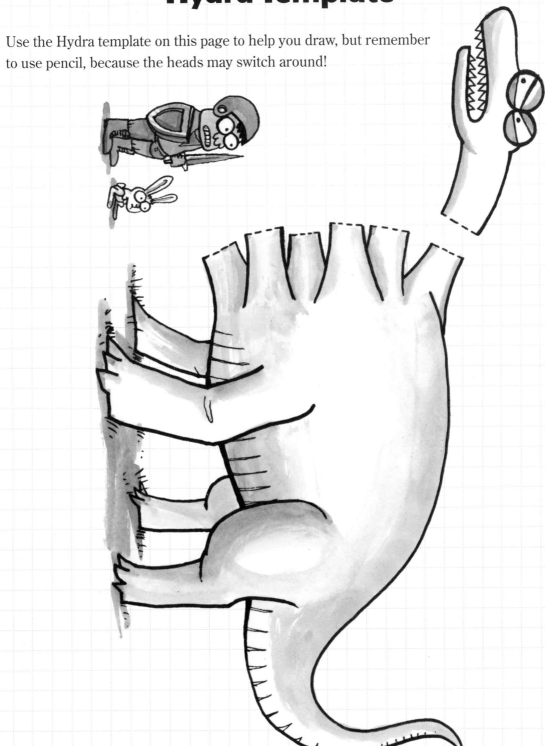

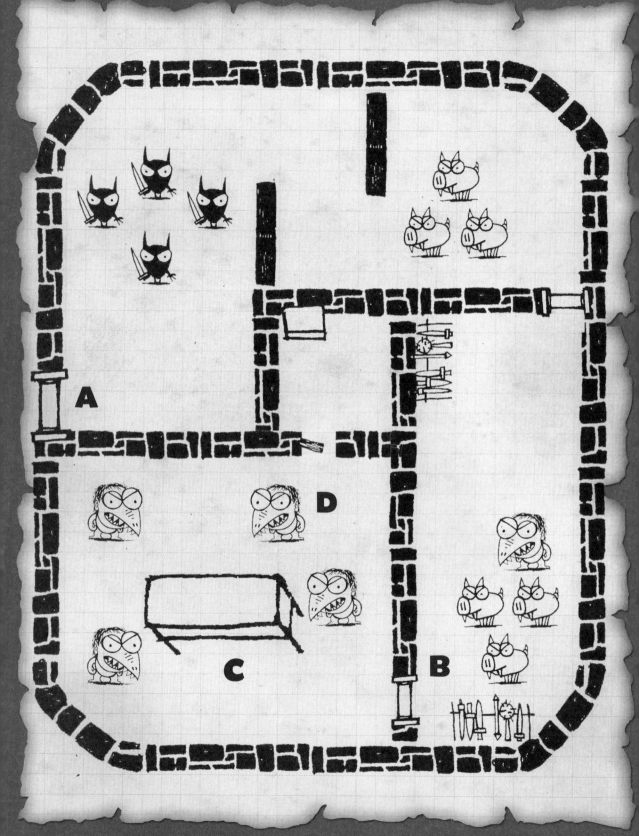

Troll Castle

Now that they've battled their way through the dangerous forest, the Heroes arrive at Troll Castle, a stronghold of those particularly nasty trolls they've just met. The castle looks like a giant drippy mud castle and has a thick stone door that must weigh several tons. In the middle of the door is a giant animated gargoyle's head. The Heroes must get inside the castle, battle these trolls, and take back some of the valuables that they have stolen.

A. The castle walls are impenetrable so the only way in is through the giant stone door with the enchanted gargoyle on it. Above the door is a plaque that says, "CATCROW." The gargoyle face is an enchanted lock that won't open until it likes what it sees. The GM may tell the players: "The gargoyle won't answer any questions but it sees all."

To solve this riddle, the Heroes must draw one animal that is the combination of the two animals. Each Hero must draw their own animal at the same time.

Pro Tip: Roll a d20 to pick two new animals to combine.
Pro Tip 2: Give out XP to Heroes with great drawings!

B. If the Heroes search for the tool rack, they will find a bunch of worthless tools and two usable items:

Hardwood Spear (Can be thrown 8 squares/40 ft)	
3 Attack Dice	1 Defense Dice

Giant Warhammer, two-handed	
5 Attack Dice	0 Defense Dice

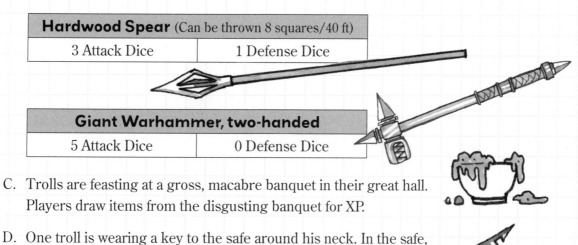

C. Trolls are feasting at a gross, macabre banquet in their great hall. Players draw items from the disgusting banquet for XP.

D. One troll is wearing a key to the safe around his neck. In the safe, there are 300 gold pieces.

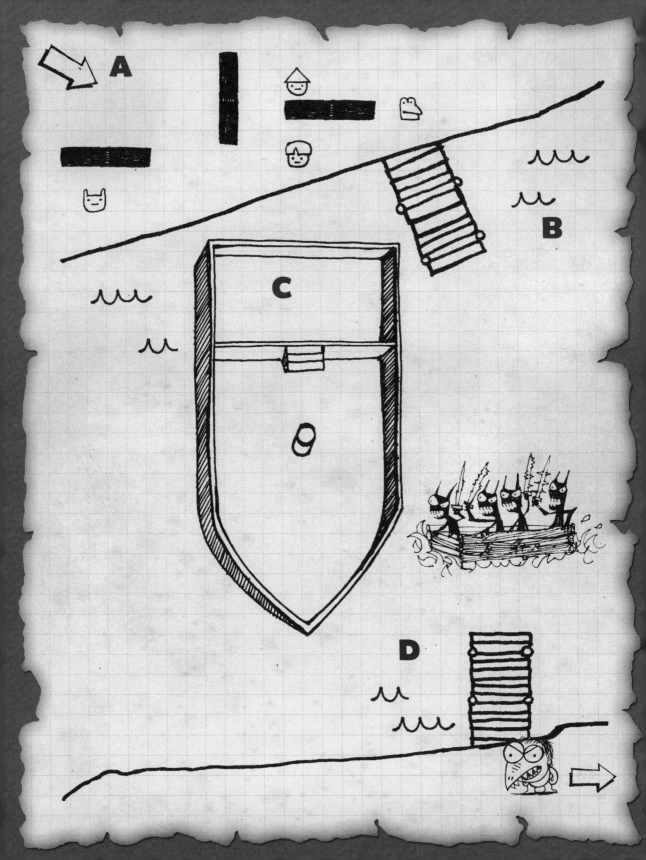

River Crossing

A raging river is in the path of the Heroes on their way to the top of Toad Island. The Heroes arrive in the port town to see many creatures fleeing the island in panic. Meanwhile, the Heroes need to find a way onto Toad Island.

A. The Heroes start by the docks and observe many boats coming from Toad Island. The GM can create random characters from the tables prior. Also, the GM should encourage the players to interview the townsfolk. Through the interviews, players learn:
   - Evil creatures are taking over the island. Most townspeople are choosing to leave.
   - The Gorgox is a dragon boss who is taking prisoners.
   - The evil spirits are coming from the top of Toad Island.
   - Edwin Tortice used to be a kind lord but now he has totally changed.

B. The last person the Heroes meet will be Captain Rolph. He has a very small ship that is making runs back and forth from the island to the mainland.
   - Rolph speaks like a salty pirate, and he is a werewolf.
   - Rolph refuses to make any more trips in his boat, unless the Heroes give up all their money, every cent. After he gets the money, he changes into a friendly werewolf.

Because he has to captain the boat, Rolph will give the Heroes an ornate harpoon gun as a gift at the start of the boatride.

Harpoon gun, two-handed	
range: 14 squares, 70 ft	6 Attack Dice
	2 harpoons

C. The Heroes must now cross the river and stay within the template of the boat until the end of the quest. Three rickety rafts full of Enemies will take turns attacking the boat in this order:

Boat 1: 6 weirdlings and 2 reptoid captains
Boat 2: 12 weirdlings, one Troll dressed as a captain
Boat 3: 5 Gritches and 3 Reptoids

D. If the Heroes stay in the water for more than one turn, summon 1d6 Krokobos on the beginning of their next turn.

Krokobos: an alligator with mouths on both ends		
4 Attack Dice	2 Defense Dice	2 HP

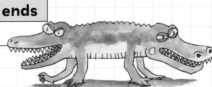

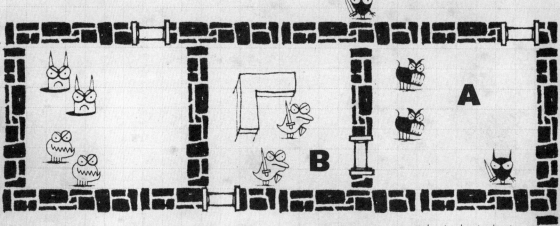

A

B

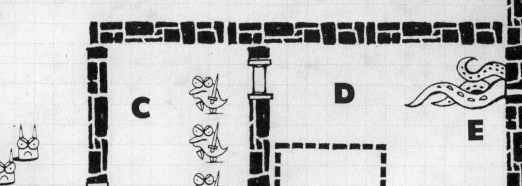

C

D

E

F

Rescue Sniffkin

The town the Heroes reach is in total chaos. The last of the citizens are trying to escape with the few belongings that they can carry. A grandma dwarf, Fleury White, rushes up to the Heroes and frantically explains that her granddaughter Sniffkin has been kidnapped by the evil Gorgox. Fleury is desperate and has been looking for a brave group of Heroes to help her.

The Heroes accept this mission because they are brave. Fleury offers the group a small, round droid to help them.

Clockwork Droid

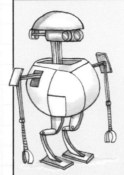

2 Attack Dice	2 Defense Dice	2 HP
Power: 6	Skill: 6	Wit: 3

The droid can retract its appendages to become a hard, dense ball. Choose a Hero to control the droid.

A. **Exotic Pet Store:** Each player draws an exotic pet for XP. If the Heroes search for secrets, they find a Poison Frog Blowdart Gun.

Poison Frog Blowdart Gun	
range: 8 squares, 40 ft	darts cause Enemy to lose two rounds

SNIFFKIN

B. **Shelf Smash Trap:** If a Hero steps here, two shelves smash together and that Hero takes 2 HP damage.

C. **Murphy's Lunch Counter:** The Heroes draw their favorite food for XP and 4 HP.

D. **Trap Door Squid:** If the Heroes step on this square, a Wild Land Squid is released from the square.

E. **Wild Land Squid, slippery**

4 attacks per turn	2 Attack Dice	1 Defense Dice	8 HP

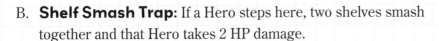

F. **Sniffkin:** When the Heroes reach this spot, they find Sniffkin in a bamboo cage on a wagon. Fleury has been following behind closely and the two cheerfully reunite. They give the group their helper droid to keep. However, Sniffkin tells the group that she was just one of many creatures that were kidnapped by the Gorgox. The Heroes' mission is not done!

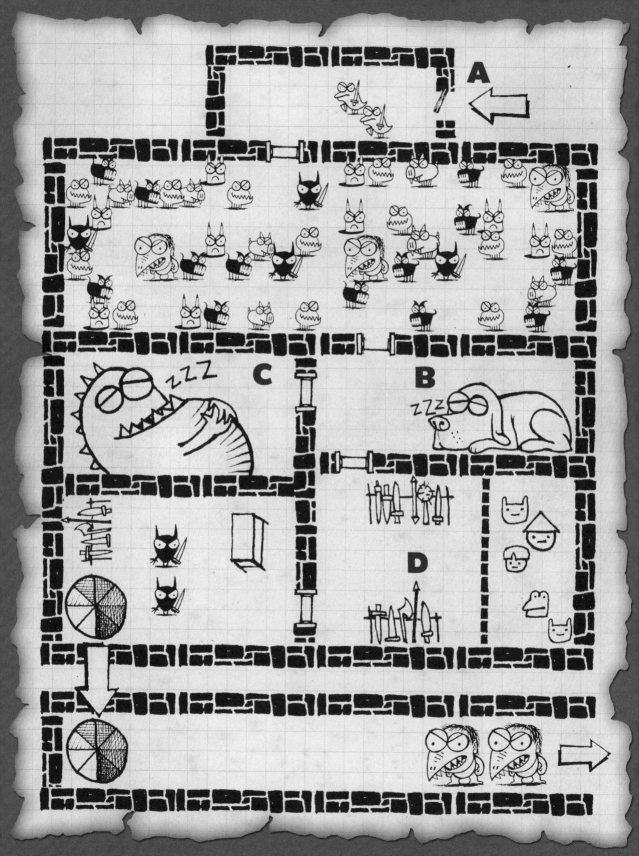

Jailbreak

The mighty, evil Gorgox has imprisoned many innocent civilians in his dark castle. The Heroes have waited until the middle of the night when all the Enemies are snoozing. They must sneak through the castle undetected and free the citizens from the basement dungeon without waking up any of their Enemies.

A. **Tiptoeing Mini Game:** Each Hero will roll 1d6 for movement in this room to simulate tiptoeing through a room of sleeping monsters. Heroes move along the series of numbers until they reach the next door. When the Hero lands on a space, they roll a d20 and add it to their Skill score to try to get that number or higher.

   Every time a Hero fails this check, the group gets a murmur token. These can also be counted by using a dice and ticking it up.

Murmur Token	Enemies Awoken
Once you get to 3 tokens, awaken 5 Weirdlings.	
4	3 Reptoid, 3 Zibble
5	4 Bork, 1 Troll
6	d20 weirdlings, d20 Gritch

B. Here lies the snoozing Inferno, the Fire Doggo and the lap dog of the Gorgox. Move through the room without awakening the beast or it will attack. Reset the murmur tokens. Inferno wakes up on the third token.

Inferno, Fire Doggo			
4 Attack Dice	5 Defense Dice	4HP	Can cast Breathe Fire once.

C. The Gorgox is sleeping inside this room, making very loud, wet snoring sounds but does not wake up until the very end of this quest.

D. The Armory of the Gorgox contains very strong weapons and the civilians, but the murmur tokens don't reset from Inferno's room. If Inferno is defeated, use the first table.

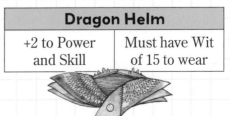

Axe of the Dragon King, two-handed		
4 Attack Dice	3 Defense Dice	Must have a power of 15 to hold

Dragon Helm	
+2 to Power and Skill	Must have Wit of 15 to wear

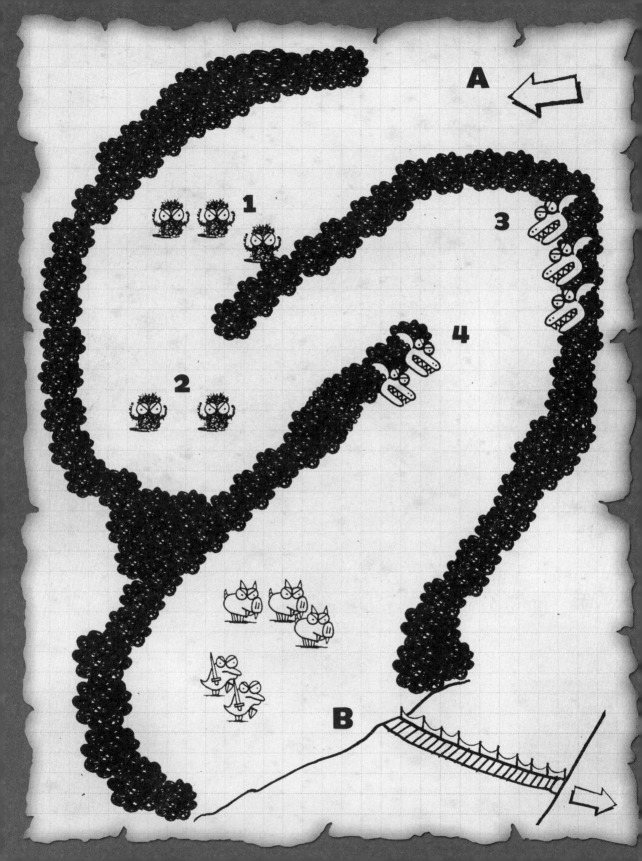

Deadly Dash

In this quest, the Heroes will be running for their lives! Gorgox, the Mystic Dragonlord, is chasing after them and will surely squash or eat them if he catches up. If the Heroes can get through the forest to the cliffs, they have a chance. "Sometimes bravery is knowing when to run."

GM note: This is a suspenseful, timed event, so maybe use a kitchen or cell phone timer to increase suspense. Cool, suspenseful music is also fun.

The Gorgox can't be beaten in regular combat with the Heroes at this point in their training. The GM can let the Heroes know this. Let the Heroes know that perhaps environmental factors can be used to slow down the Gorgox. If the Heroes persist in fighting directly with the Gorgox, use these stats:

Gorgox, level 12 Dragonlord		
10 Attack Dice	10 Defense Dice	20 HP

A. Heroes roll for initiative, determining the order for the entire quest. Then, each Hero will move using 2d6 instead of their normal movement stat. The Gorgox will move seven spaces a round. If it reaches a Hero, it will immediately attack.

Obstacles: Using environmental elements to slow down the Gorgox is the Heroes' best option.

1. A barrel of acorn oil
2. An abandoned carriage full of luggage
3. A coil of scratchy rope, 100 feet
4. A two-handed axe stuck into a tree

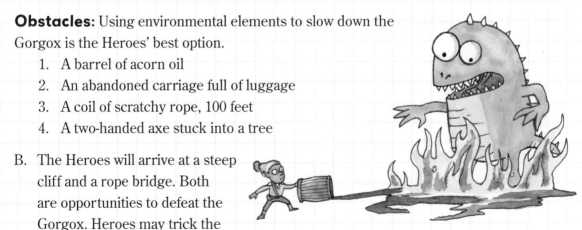

B. The Heroes will arrive at a steep cliff and a rope bridge. Both are opportunities to defeat the Gorgox. Heroes may trick the Gorgox into falling off the cliff or they may lure the Gorgox across the rope bridge and cut the ropes. The rope bridge has an HP of 8.

Toad Island Mystics

After the Heroes fled to safety, the Gorgox could not avoid the steep cliff! The remaining citizens are so thankful the Gorgox is gone, they reveal the location of two hidden sages that may be able to help the Heroes on their Quest to face Edwin Tortice. The only way to go is up, so they're going to need to use the airship.

The Airship

The Island of the Mystics is floating in free air hundreds of feet above Toad Island. Luckily, the townsfolk are so grateful that the Gorgox is gone, one of them is willing to give you a ride. Their name is Chester Green and they happen to have one of the best airships in the whole region. All aboard! However, you will have to get past some unsavory characters on the way up.

The Heroes will spend this whole quest on Chester's airship as it ascends to The Island of the Mystics. Three waves of Enemies will attack the ship and the Heroes inside. The Heroes must repel all the Enemies in order to get to the floating island.

Wave I. Borks with Wings. Roll 2d6 for amount of Flying Borks. Watch out! Borks have sharp tusks!

Wave II. Weirldlings in Heli-Thopters. Roll 1d20 for amount of Weirdlings. A group of surly weirdlings attack the ship. Use your best pirate impression as the rickety, makeshift thopters surround Chester's airship.

Wave III. Grells Psychic Attack. The air around the Heroes becomes hazy and purple as mysterious Grells surround the airship. They won't attack the Heroes with weapons, but with a psychic attack.

After each Hero is attacked by a grell, the Heroes win the quest and arrive at Mystic Island.

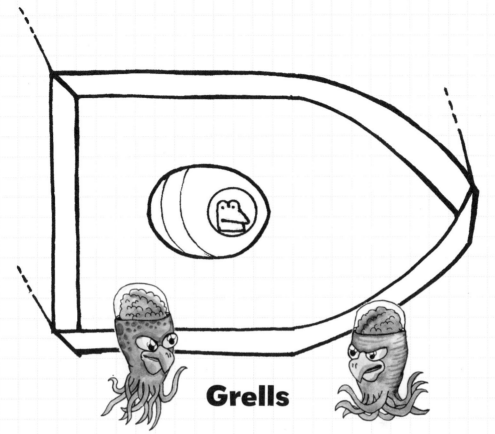

Grells

Grells are otherworldly, floating squids that attack with their brains.

Psychic Attack: The GM will make random, wild scribbles, maybe even with their eyes closed. Other players can also donate wild scribbles.

When a Hero is "attacked," the GM will give them one of these wild scribbles, and by continuing the drawing, they will turn the scribble into a drawing of a certain animal. The GM can use the Familiars table on page 75.

Go around the table a couple times with different scribbles. When each player has done a successful drawing, the challenge of the Grells is over, the purple clouds recede, and the Grells float away.

Once the challenges are over, the Heroes land on the Island of the Mystics. Chester Green gives the Heroes a present for their next quest.

Personal Helium Balloon: A small, stitched, leather pouch with a ripcord that inflates into a ballon, causing it to rise slowly 100 feet into the air. The balloon has four handles for the Heroes to hold onto.

Gallopi Gus

Gallopi Gus is an ancient, blind turtleman who will put the Heroes through a series of games that will test their senses but not their weapons.

A. This is an ambush! Once all the Heroes pass these Enemies, attack them from the back!

B. If the Heroes search the Zat's nest, they find four items from the treasure table and an Amulet of Charisma. The wearer of the amulet can roll 2d20 when trying to persuade any enemy.

C. When the Heroes meet Gallopi Gus, he is drawing in a giant, smooth sandbox with a gnarled staff. His eyes have long since sunken and disappeared. He says, "A true Hero must be able to rely on their strengths as well as their weaknesses, because they never know when a sense could be taken away." When Gus says the last two words, one Hero goes completely blind (pick one), and the game begins.

Blind Drawing Mini Game

1. Heroes take turns covering their eyes. The Hero will roll a d20 and the GM will whisper a clue in their ear.

2. Now the blinded player must silently draw the clue and the other Heroes will have to guess the clue. The GM uses the tables here or their own ideas.

When each Hero has completed this challenge, Gallopi Gus gives the Heroes a group challenge.

1	bow & arrow	roots	key
2	rope	glove	toilet
3	T. rex	eyeball	farm
4	kiss	handstand	spaceship
5	axe	forest	flower
6	moon	earth	umbrella
7	king	clown	watermelon
8	river	crossbow	sweat
9	angel	pig	read
10	dream	squirrel	dolphin
11	castle	surfing	keyboard
12	guitar	palm tree	pyramid
13	shark	dog	pizza
14	sew	cat	igloo
15	chain	juggle	lips
16	horse	dessert	giraffe
17	rain	submarine	yawn
18	bee	shield	corn
19	hammer	volcano	snow
20	pregnant	parrot	turtle

Whisper Train/Secret Phrase

Gallopi Gus is prepared to give the group a mystic weapon for their mission, but it is locked in one of three chests. Gallopi Gus will utter a clue to the first Hero, and then that Hero must whisper the clue to the next Hero, and it goes down the line until the last Hero. The last Hero must open the correct chest without any more help from the other Heroes. The whispered phrase should use alliteration and/or rhyming to be a little confusing. For example:

"Splish Splash is a slippery water river bath."

"High in the bright blue sky with a bird's flying eye."

"Sneaking Sammy squeaks, cheese please."

The chest contains the Turtle Spike.

Turtle Spike			
3 Attack Dice	3 Defense Dice	One Handed	Can be activated to extend to poke or pierce up to 15 feet. Turtle Spike must reset for one turn after activating.

The Tree of Zats

The other Mystic that the group must reach lives atop an epically large tree that happens to be full of cantankerous zats. The Heroes must reach the top and complete another series of brain challenges to get the next mystic item.

On this game board, the the group takes turns using 1d6 to "climb" up the tree. If they land on a space that intersects with the leaves of the tree, they disturb a nest of zats, and the Heroes have to fight with them immediately. At the top, they reach Byron Blink's castle and must complete two challenges.

Byron Blink's Fleeting Image

Byron Blink is a powerful chameleon Mystic that can change into any color or pattern or even disappear at will. He poses a drawing challenge called "Fleeting Image," also known as "Picture Telephone."

1. The game starts with the GM doing a small, one-minute drawing on a small slip of paper. The GM can use the many drawing idea tables throughout this book. For example, say the GM wanted to incorporate: SHARK/KISS/RIVER/DREAM, the GM might draw the top drawing shown here.

2. The GM then reveals the drawing to the first Hero, but only for three seconds!

3. That Hero now has a minute to redraw the drawing to the best of their memory. When they are done, they show it to the next Hero, but only for three seconds.

4. Each Hero gets a chance to draw. At the end, the Heroes compare the very last drawing to the GM's drawing to see how close they are.

There are no losers in this game; it's just fun to see the drawings change. After the Heroes complete this challenge, Byron still isn't convinced, and he makes them do one more challenge.

PLAYER ONE SEES THIS ↑ DRAWS THIS ↓

PLAYER TWO SEES THIS ↑ DRAWS THIS ↓

PLAYER THREE SEES THIS ↑ DRAWS THIS ↓

. . . AND SO ON . . .

Summon a Phantasm

Once the Heroes complete the Fleeting Image challenge, Byron Blink will have them complete another drawing challenge. Byron wants to give the Heroes a mystic artifact, but he needs to summon a spirit that will conjure your reward from another dimension. To do this, the Heroes will complete a collaborative drawing called "Summon a Phantasm," also known as "Exquisite Corpse."

A. Divide a piece of paper into four parts, and each Hero will draw a different section of a figure without looking at the other sections. As the group moves along, the GM will fold the paper so that the other areas are hidden. Use the drawing tables if stumped!

B. Like Fleeting Image, there are no losers in this game. If the Heroes complete the task, even abstractly, Byron says he is pleased with the way they use teamwork and gives them the mystic artifact.

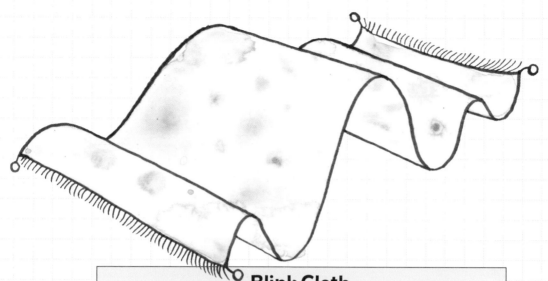

Blink Cloth,
a mystic artifact made by Byron Blink

Heroes under the cloth can't be seen by Enemy creatures.
This item can be carried without taking up any space.
6 ft x 4 ft cloth, can hide 1–3 Heroes depending on size.

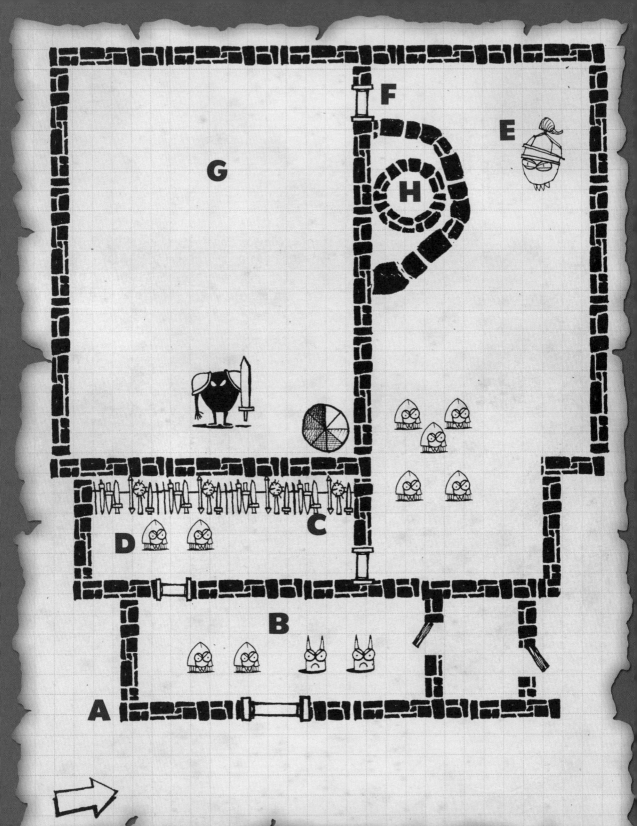

Castle Tortice

Atop Toad Island is the dark and foreboding castle of Lord Edwin Tortice. The Heroes can hear the forlorn cries of the moon drake Tazzaphur and see a sickly purple glow radiating from the castle's cracks. The Heroes have battled many Enemies, acquired powerful weapons, and gained valuable experience. They are ready to rescue Tazz!

A. A secret side passage inside the castle.

B. Pit Trap: Fallen Heroes take 2 HP damage and find two Borks at the bottom.

C. Weapons Trap: If the Heroes grab without searching, they find the weapons spring-loaded and take 2 HP damage. They can find a:

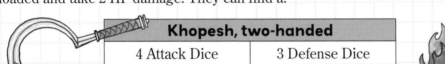

Khopesh, two-handed	
4 Attack Dice	3 Defense Dice

D. These are Fire Scorpies, impervious to fire and fire spells. They attack as normal but with hot coal shovels and can toss hot coals four squares or 20 feet for 1d6 damage.

E. **Scorpy Lord**

4 Attack Dice	4 Defense Dice	4 HP	10 squares or 50 feet movement	Three Spells: Fear, Summon d6 Scorpy, Fireball

If searched after the battle, the Scorpy Lord carried a tub of salve which will heal the Heroes a combined 8 HP.

F. This is a thick wooden door with a DL of 22 and 10 HP. Heroes can hear the screeches of Tazzaphur beyond the door. It must be smashed.

G. This is the chamber of Edwin Tortice.

H. This is a spiral staircase leading to the top of Castle Tortice. Heroes can see a powerful purple glow emanating down the staircase. They can hear Tazzaphur screeching and struggling above.

Edwin Tortice, Turtle Lord

When the Heroes enter the final chamber of the castle, Edwin Tortice, the Turtle Lord, beckons to them:

"Not long ago, I was a humble steward and common metalsmith, satisfied to make simple weapons for normal Heroes. But then a strange traveler came to me and taught me how to use powerful dark magic that gave me immense power. Now that I have all the power, I take what I want. I took the citizens as prisoners, and I took their land and weapons. I took the moon drake. And now, I will take you . . . AND CHOP YOU IN HALF!"

A. Edwin Tortice is wearing two enchanted turtles as shoulder pads or Totem Armor, and it turns out these turtles love charades. The GM will prepare a clue for each Shoulder Turtle from the d20 tables in this book, or perhaps use the title of a TV show, movie, or book. This clue is given secretly to one Hero, and they must silently act out the clue until the other Heroes guess it correctly, and one Shoulder Turtle pops off Edwin Tortice.

A

B. After the Totem Armor is gone, the Heroes can battle Edwin as normal. Edwin's sword's name is "Sir Choppington" and has a range of three squares or 15 feet.

B

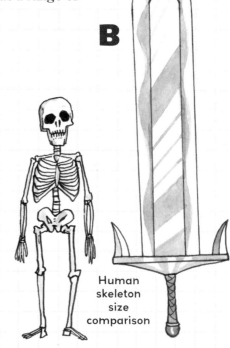

Human skeleton size comparison

Edwin Tortice, corrupted Dark Turtle Lord			
8 Attack Dice	4 Defense Dice	15 squares movement	10 HP

C. When finally defeated, Edwin Tortice returns to his normal, human size. He is confused and doesn't remember the fight that just occurred at all. Edwin does suggest that the Heroes take his sword, "Sir Choppington." The sword is so large and heavy, it requires a Power score of 24 to handle. This will require two Heroes. The Heroes should proceed up the staircase toward the purple light and the cries of the moon drake.

The Battle for Toad Island

After the Heroes defeat Edwin Tortice, they ascend the staircase. Now they are on the top of the castle that is at the very top of the island. From this viewpoint, they can now see the truth. The very island itself is a giant, enchanted toad. All this activity and combat has roused the toad from hibernation, and now the group has attracted its attention. The giant toad attacks the Heroes as they stand atop Toad Island.

The Top of Toad Island

A. The Heroes start by coming out of the stairs, one-by-one.

B. This is a tall smokestack, billowing dark smoke.

C. This is a purple energy dome, with Tazzaphur and a purple crystal underneath. No normal weapons can pierce the dome.

D. All the Enemies must be cleared from the top of Toad Island to complete this portion of the quest.

E. Once cleared, the giant toad will attack the Heroes until they can figure out the puzzle of the purple dome. Turn to the next page for the description of the Toad's attacks.

Toad Island Attacks

When it is the Toad Island's turn to attack, the GM can do so one of two ways: a Tongue Strike or a Thundering Ribbit.

Tongue Strike

- The GM folds a paper airplane.
- The GM rolls a d6 to see how many feet away from the table they have to stand.
- The GM throws the paper airplane to represent the tongue striking.
- If a Hero is hit, that Hero loses half their life, rounded down (e.g., 13 HP loses 6 life).

Thundering Ribbit

With this attack, imagine that the toad is taking a huge, deep breath of air and producing a croak that is more rattling than a thunderstorm.

- Heroes and Enemies are both affected.
- Enemies lose a turn for each Defense Dice they have.
- Heroes each roll a d6 and must move their figure that many spaces away from where they were.

Solving the Puzzle

It is completely impossible to hurt the toad. It's just too huge. The toad can only be calmed by destroying the purple crystal. However, no weapon the Heroes have can damage or breach the energy dome that is protecting the crystal and imprisoning the moon drake Tazzaphur.

The only thing that can penetrate the magical purple energy is the Blink Cloth.

Two Heroes must hold up the Blink Cloth, creating a hole in the energy dome. Then the Heroes must use Sir Choppington, the Turtle Spike, Harpoon Gun, or other improvised tool to knock over the dome generator.

Once the crystal is dislodged from the energy shield generator, the force field will dissipate, and the moon drake Tazzaphur will be released. If the Heroes need help figuring out this puzzle, give them some clues after Wit checks.

The moon drake has been freed from the energy field, but the Heroes must destroy the crystal to make the turtle stop attacking. Hitting the crystal with any normal weapon will destroy the Hero's weapon.

The crystal can only be thrown into the furnace or smashed by Sir Choppington. Sir Choppington is so large, it takes a combined strength of 24 to hold and swing the giant sword, meaning two Heroes will need to hold it.

Once the crystal is shattered, the giant toad grunts and returns to the sea.

Return of the Magician

Just as the purple haze dissipates and the toad's head settles under the ocean's surface, the magician and the unidonkey suddenly appear, streaking from the sky.

Lars Depple had been faking the whole time! The magician and his stead were much more powerful than they revealed before.

Lars dismounts from his unidonkey, Hank Saturday, and starts to give his evil-villain monologue.

Depple's Backstory

Lars Depple loved animals. He loved them too much. He loved capturing and keeping animals in cages and in chains and controlling them. As a child, he had an extensive collection of pets, some legal and some not. He read a lot of books and studied spells and excelled in magical pursuits in school.

Lars was so talented, he was offered a teaching position at Sherrywood Forest, Institute for Heroes, by WynWyn herself, but Lars turned the job down. He craved more power and instead traveled the world, learning more about the powerful dark arts and meeting sinister warlocks and witches.

Lars concentrated his powers on attracting animals and controlling them to do his will. Eventually, Lars focused his attention on a creature so large, it was as big as an island.

So, when Lars Depple saw the opportunity, he betrayed a fellow poacher and stole a powerful Crystal of Control and set out to use it against the toad that was as big as an island.

But when he found Lord Edwin Tortice atop Toad Island already, Lars Depple thought he found a good opportunity to obtain one of his most sought-after Familiars, the moon drake. He would use dark magic mind control to have Edwin Tortice steal the drake for him, while keeping his own hands clean.

But now the Heroes have ruined the plans of Lars Depple. He is furious. Lars was on the cusp of controlling one of the largest toads on the planet, and now his precious crystal has been destroyed! Lars demands retribution! And now, an epic showdown ensues.

Image Scrimmage

The battle with the magician takes place using your most powerful trait and the most magical part of your brain: your imagination. This is NOT a game of who can draw better, but who can think fast and compete with their ideas. Image Scrimmage is a competition drawing game of wits. It is a game where ideas and creatures compete in one-upmanship.

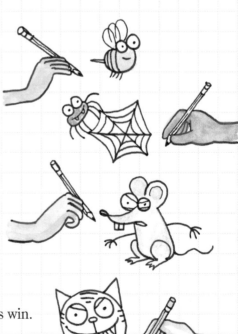

Here's how it works:

1. Players draw on one piece of paper, or simply use their imaginations without paper.

2. Take turns among drawings that compete with each other. Start small and take logical steps forward. If the first person draws a mouse, the obvious response could be a cat.

3. This is a game where you draw or describe anything (animal, feeling, emotion, object, happening, event, nouns, verbs, etc.) that would be better or defeat the last thing, physically or mentally.

4. The best, most clever, most epic, most creative solutions are the winning solutions in this game. Admit defeat when you've been defeated.

5. Clever and creative narrative surprises always win.

6. Everyone picks the winner together.

7. Most importantly, have fun!

Image Scrimmage Example

A. A gnarly stag beetle
B. A stinging scorpion
C. A sneaky chameleon
D. A terrible pterodactyl
E. A gargantuan T. rex
F. Ulmog the Beast from Beyond
G. Snuggles, the world's cutest kitten, who can melt the heart of even the cruelest villain

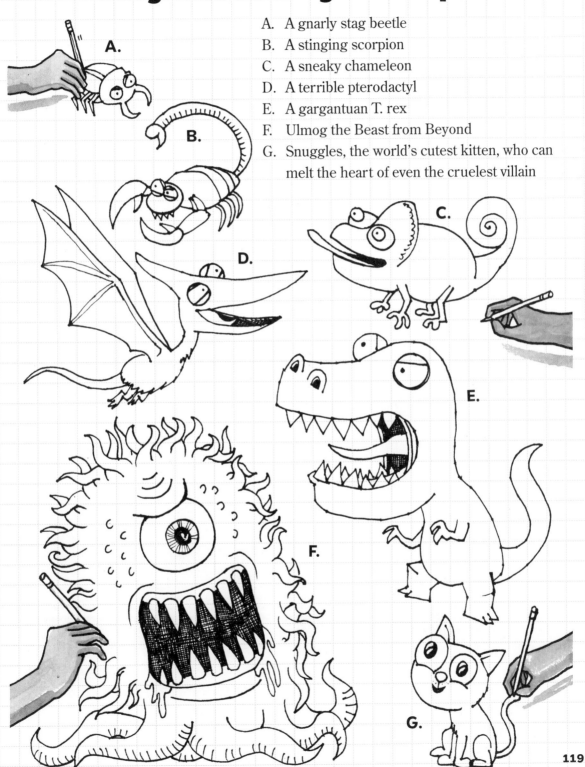

THE CONCLUSION

Players will battle Lars Depple, the dark magician, until they have sufficiently defeated him in Image Scrimmage. The Heroes must work together to be funny, devastating, clever, and surprising to win this battle of wits. The GM may want to battle the players in Image Scrimmage more than once.

Mentally bettered and morally defeated, the magician admits his loss. Lars hastily pulls Hank Saturday, and, with a rainbow fart, the pair quickly fly far away.

The Heroes have defeated a terrible evil force and freed the beloved school mascot, Tazzaphur, the moon drake. Many more adventures await the Heroes, but for now they return to Sherrywood Forest triumphant. Tazzaphur is now available as a Familiar for the Heroes.

Tazzaphur

Mystic Familiar/moon drake

+3 Skill and Wit	Gives one Hero telekinesis up to half of that Hero's weight	**RW:** Gives invincibility for 1d6 rounds.

Glossary

Action—Anything that a Hero can do. Searching for secrets, casting a spell, healing a friend, and many more actions are listed in the "How to Role-Play" section.

Adjacent—Right next to; the closest.

Advantage—When you roll with advantage, you roll with two dice and choose the better one.

Attack—When your Hero attacks an Enemy, you will roll one or more d6 dice.

Backstory—This is what happened to the Heroes before the campaign.

Campaign—A longer role-playing story that takes multiple quests to finish.

Catchphrase—A saying that a Hero can say over and over again that helps to emphasize the character's personality.

Character—Each player will create a character that represents them in the role-playing game. A character is also called a Hero.

Character Sheet—A piece of paper where the players will keep track of their character's items and abilities.

Character Type—This is the type of creature you are. This is commonly called "race" in other RPGs.

Combat—When Heroes and Enemies battle each other.

Dice/Die—You roll them for random numbers. *Scales & Tales* uses d6 and d20 dice.

Enemy—Foes the Heroes might battle or outwit on their adventure.

Experience Points (XP)—Points representing merits that the GM awards Heroes when they are especially creative.

Familiar—Animal friends that aid Heroes.

Game Master (GM)—This person is in charge of telling the story and guiding players through quests and acting as all the Enemies and side characters.

Guardian—A healer, fighter, and spellcaster in one. A versatile Hero Type, also known as a Cleric in other RPGs.

Hero—Each player will create and play the game as a Hero.

Hero Trait—Everything in the *Scales & Tales* world can be tested against Power, Skill, and Wit.

Hero Type—There are four standard Hero Types: Guardian, Rogue, Warrior, and Wizard.

Hit Points (HP)—The amount of life a Hero or Enemy has.

Hydra—A flightless dragon with many heads.

Initiative—Order of turns. When rolling for initiative, all players roll a d20 and take turns in that order, highest to lowest.

Miniature—When role-playing on a tabletop, miniatures are little figures that represent Heroes, Enemies, and other creatures and characters.

Mystic—A very special type of rare creature imbued with magic.

Party—A group of Heroes.

Quest—An adventure that should take the span of a night of gaming.

Range—How far a weapon can fire a projectile.

Ranged—This means a weapon can shoot something from a distance away.

Scrimmage—A battle or duel.

Static—Something staying still or staying put.

Terrain—Anything that would restrict the movement of the Heroes, including walls, doors, trees, water, etc.

World Building—When a GM creates a detailed environment where players can role-play, often involving a storyline that leads them through the setting.

Treasure

There are some points during the game when it makes sense to reward a Hero, or the party may find a treasure chest or search an Enemy. Use this table to award random treasure. These treasures don't have descriptions, but that is part of the fun. The GM can write the descriptions or let the players write their own descriptions.

Does the artifact improve a Hero Trait? Does it have a one-time use? Does it have a disadvantage as well as advantages? The only rule is to make it fair, so it doesn't throw the whole game out of balance.

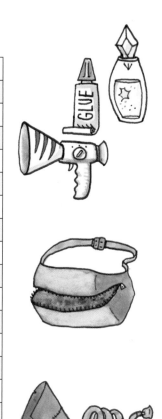

1	Beetle brooch
2	Robe of beautiful colors
3	Wand of fire
4	Eye of charming
5	Animated rope
6	Super adhesive gel
7	Potion of life
8	Bag of tricks
9	Cone of collapse
10	Bottomless fanny pack
11	Feather of falling
12	Bag of beans
13	Scarab of Death
14	Spectacles of the Artificer
15	Fang of Kaag
16	Bubble Horn
17	Golden Quill
18	Endless Watering Can
19	Figurine of Awesome Power
20	Incredible Cookie

Scrolls

Spellcasters, like Wizards and Guardians, can cast a scroll for free, as an action.

For a Rogue or Warrior to cast a spell from a scroll, they must roll a d20 to test their Wit or Skill against a difficulty level of 15.

Succeed or fail, the scroll crumbles after one use.

1, 2	Sleep: Pick an Enemy your character can see. That Enemy loses 1d6 turns.
3, 4	Levitate: Hero floats 10 feet above ground. Enemies lose 1 Defense Dice when attacking. Ends when Hero takes damage.
5, 6	Revive: Target Hero returns to the HP they started the quest with.
7, 8	Explode: The scroll goes on a ten second countdown and then explodes, dealing 3 damage to each creature in a 4 square (20-foot) radius.
9, 10	Fireball: The scroll turns into a fireball the size of a softball able to be thrown. Deal 2 damage to any target you can hit with this fireball.
11, 12	Warp: Return to a place you have been before or teleport to any place you can see.
13, 14	Hole: After reading, the scroll adheres to a wall or floor and becomes a hole.
15, 16	Mirror Image: Creates a mirrored phantasm of the Hero. Ends when damage is dealt to the true Hero.
17, 18	Gust of Wind: An immense squall blows through the area, sweeping 1d6 Enemies 6 spaces (30 feet) away.
19, 20	Bubble: A protective energy bubble appears around the Hero in a 10-foot radius. Bubble pops when dealt damage.

Name Generator

What you see on this page is a chart that may be able to help you choose a brand-new name for your Hero character. Remember, the most memorable names are short and sweet.

So	Az	Bi	Co	Da	Fi	Eck	Ga	Hy	Ip	Ku	Lo
Do	Whip	Buck	Bold	Crud	Me	Von	Swift	Count	Rod	Sir	Me
Ge	Mind	Wood	Queen	Gar	Val	Jonny	Mag	Tal	Jar	Dar	Na
Ki	Jes	Cha	Trol	Med	Krys	Ton	Lean	Dok	Berk	Kor	Er
Le	Van	Terr	Lard	Claw	Brite	Atta	Dia	Nick	Clay	Biz	Ot
Ma	Clav	Brind	Flink	Biff	Tieg	Xix	Tina	Ha	Mer	Gubb	Pa
Ni	Lord	Room	King	Zoob	Ard	Reve	Zil	Oight	Soul	Mor	Qui
Pe	Lig	Biby	Pin	Bink	Rome	Beeb	Dov	Swom	Wap	Gorn	El
Ri	Rust	Xeeb	Qirk	Rory	Zarb	Priago	Jero	Muff	Fizz	Cheez	Ru
Sa	To	Va	Ep	Wi	Za	Zu	Ya	Wo	Vi	Um	Ta

Difficulty Level

When you make a skill check or test your Hero Trait, you roll a d20 and add it to your Hero Trait score: either Power, Skill, or Wit.

11–15	Cracking a walnut Carefully opening a creaky door Making a good piece of toast Fixing a bike Riding a horse Catching a fish
16–18	Reading a foreign language Fixing a boat's hull Sneaking past guards Driving a motor vehicle Catching a cat Haggling with a merchant
19–22	Deciphering a lost language Fluent in three languages Making Hollandaise sauce Fixing an old motor Opening a door that's rusted shut Catching a boar
23–26	Holding a 10-foot sword Throat singing Speaking an ancient language Fixing any motor vehicle Flying an air vehicle Taming a horse
27–30	Breaching a Dark Lord's Armor Deciphering an alien language Cyber-hacking Fixing a spaceship Piercing an Elder Dragon's scales Catching a trillopede

Campaign Generator

Someday you might want to start your own multi-quest campaign! Use these d20 tables or write your own.

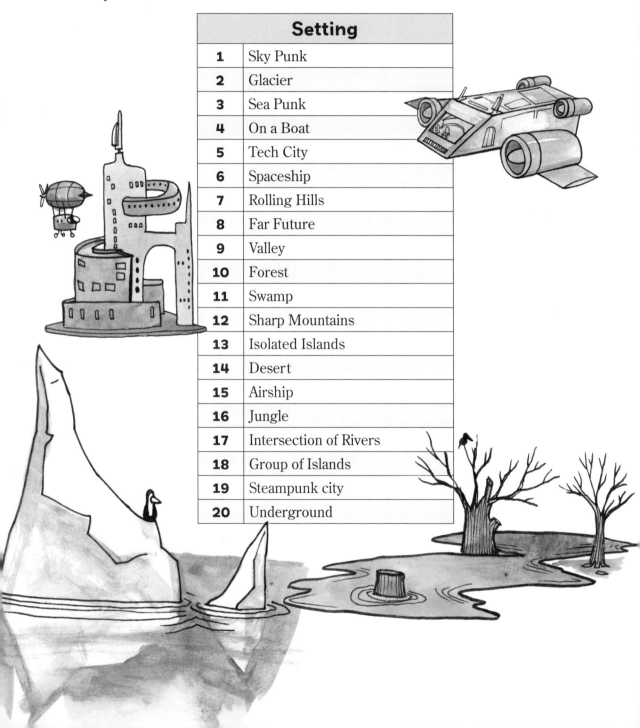

	Setting
1	Sky Punk
2	Glacier
3	Sea Punk
4	On a Boat
5	Tech City
6	Spaceship
7	Rolling Hills
8	Far Future
9	Valley
10	Forest
11	Swamp
12	Sharp Mountains
13	Isolated Islands
14	Desert
15	Airship
16	Jungle
17	Intersection of Rivers
18	Group of Islands
19	Steampunk city
20	Underground

Castle or Dungeon

1, 2	Crystal Spire
3, 4	Icy Bastion
5, 6	Howling Mine
7, 8	Labyrinth of Stone
9, 10	Wind's Wrath
11, 12	City of Gates
13, 14	Mud Manor
15, 16	Fist of the Forest
17, 18	Ocean's End
19, 20	Mountain Mirage

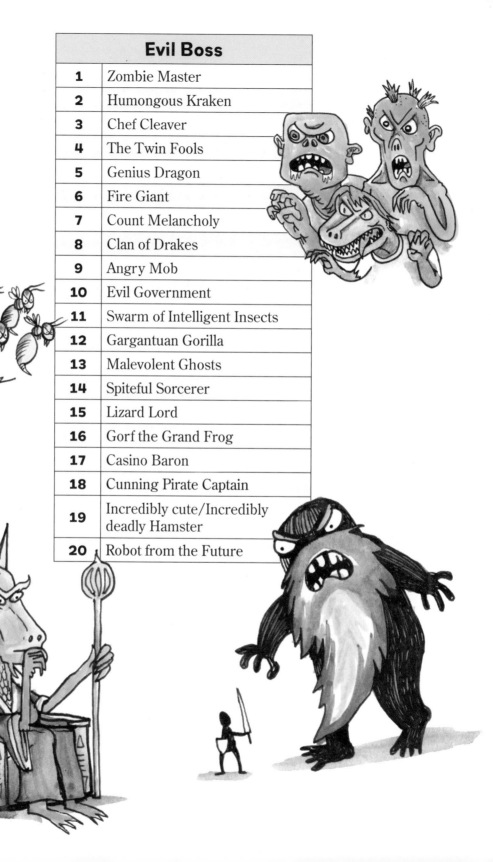

Evil Boss	
1	Zombie Master
2	Humongous Kraken
3	Chef Cleaver
4	The Twin Fools
5	Genius Dragon
6	Fire Giant
7	Count Melancholy
8	Clan of Drakes
9	Angry Mob
10	Evil Government
11	Swarm of Intelligent Insects
12	Gargantuan Gorilla
13	Malevolent Ghosts
14	Spiteful Sorcerer
15	Lizard Lord
16	Gorf the Grand Frog
17	Casino Baron
18	Cunning Pirate Captain
19	Incredibly cute/Incredibly deadly Hamster
20	Robot from the Future

A Twist	
1	King and Queen need an escort
2	All mirrors are portals
3	Unicorns are evil
4	Stuck in a loop
5	A senile warlock
6	A twisted song leads children away
7	Find a map to a dungeon
8	Asked to deliver a sealed box
9	An island appears
10	A troll won't let anyone leave
11	Random items become alive
12	Must retrieve a dragon scale for an antidote
13	Everyone in town disappears
14	Everything is a mirage
15	Thick fog coming from one direction
16	Caves and holes open up everywhere
17	Starts raining and never stops.
18	A giant vine grows into the clouds
19	The birds start speaking
20	Dinosaurs migrate through your town

So, gather some friends or friends-to-be, acquire some snacks, prepare your game board, and enjoy the role-playing!

Gaming Grid

Game Elements

Note: Make copies of this page before you cut it!

Blank Tables

1	
2	
3	
4	
5	
6	
7	
8	
9	
10	
11	
12	
13	
14	
15	
16	
17	
18	
19	
20	

1	
2	
3	
4	
5	
6	
7	
8	
9	
10	
11	
12	
13	
14	
15	
16	
17	
18	
19	
20	

1	
2	
3	
4	
5	
6	

1	
2	
3	
4	
5	
6	